WELC
TO
PAF

Rebecca

Poems from *Talking Poetry*

Edited by Susan Roberts
Introduced by Nicola Davies
and Simon Rae

BBC CHILDREN'S BOOKS

Published by BBC Books,
a division of BBC Enterprises Limited,
Woodlands, 80 Wood Lane,
London W12 0TT

First published 1993

ISBN 0 563 36482 3

Illustrations by John Bendall-Brunello

Set in Times Roman by Phoenix Photosetting, Chatham
Printed and bound in England by Clays plc, St Ives
Cover printed by Clays plc, St Ives

CONTENTS

INTRODUCTION

Alice didn't get much of a welcome when she stumbled across a tea-party in Wonderland. 'No room, no room!' cried the March Hare and the Mad Hatter as they spread themselves along the huge table. When she was finally allowed to sit down (having avoided the sleeping Dormouse), she was immediately invited to pick up her teacup and 'move one place on'. It was a very curious party.

Alice's party in Wonderland has a lot in common with the poetry party in this book. You won't find a Mad Hatter here, but you will find surprises on every page. Poetry can be curious too, it can also be dramatic; it can summon a hurricane, call up a carnival, colour a grey world and even invite the Incredible Hulk to tea.

Welcome to the Party is the second collection of poems from the *Talking Poetry* radio series, following on from *I'd like to be a Teabag*, a companion to the first series. Every week the programme follows a different theme. Each of the ten chapters in this book contains a selection of poems from one programme in the second series. It begins, as every good party should, with Celebration.

We've been doing a bit of celebrating ourselves this year. As well as the continuing success of the radio programme, we organized the first *Talking Poetry* Festival, which was held in Bristol in May. Many of the poets whose poems you'll find here came along to read and perform their work, including Kit Wright, Benjamin Zephaniah, Grace Nichols, Brian Patten and Roger McGough. We hope to run more festivals in the future and may even come to your area – so watch out for us.

Before I hand over to our equivalent of Alice and the March Hare, *Talking Poetry's* presenters Nicola Davies and

5

Simon Rae, for their thoughts on the themes in this collection, I'd just like to say 'Welcome to the Party' – we've saved the best seat for you.

Susan Roberts
Editor, *Talking Poetry*

PS: In his introduction, Simon gives us his thoughts on Celebrations, Heroes and Heroines, War, the Weather and School. Nicola shares a few ideas she's had about Colour, Travel, Cities, Wildfowl and, finally, Birth and Death. When you're reading through the poems in this book, why don't you jot down some of the thoughts which come into your head and try to turn them into a poem? If you're pleased with the result, send it to:

TALKING POETRY
BBC BROADCASTING HOUSE
WHITELADIES ROAD
BRISTOL
BS8 2LR

I would like to thank all the poets who have been involved with Talking Poetry *since its inception in September 1990, the children and schools taking part in the poetry workshops, and the poets who have contributed to this book.*
My thanks also go to the performers, to the many volunteers – including my mother, and to everyone else who helped make the Talking Poetry *Festival a success.*
Last, but not least, I'd like to thank Viv Beeby, Lorna Baker, Sarah Foster, Nick and Simon for their invaluable work on the series.

Susan Roberts

CELEBRATIONS

CELEBRATIONS

> Welcome to the party,
> welcome to the fun . . .

A party is perhaps the most obvious kind of celebration – a birthday party, an engagement party, an end-of-exams party – just a party. A party shows a generous instinct. As Robert Fisher puts it in 'Funny Folk':

> We're having a party . . .
> so come on in.

Some celebrations are more private. Zoë Gardner's poem lists a number of things that might be cause for celebration (along with one or two that won't be).

Weddings are the biggest celebrations in most people's lives. All those guests, beautifully dressed bridesmaids, the big car, the bossy photographer, confetti, exploding corks and thousands of sandwiches . . . Actually the girl in Gareth Owen's poem 'Wedding Day' is just pretending, but you can see she's imagined most of the details for herself. It's going to be a day to remember.

What other sorts of celebrations are there? All sorts, social, religious, sporting. Who wouldn't celebrate when his or her team won the cup, be it the FA Cup, or the local basketball cup?

In Max Fatchen's 'Dragon Dance', it's the Chinese New Year that's being celebrated. There's a similar carnival atmosphere in Julie Holder's 'From Carnival to Cabbages and Rain'. Everyone takes to the street – to celebrate what? Simply the joy of being alive:

> The narrow streets
> Are smiles wide
> Carnival has come to town.
> Granny has a rose in her teeth
> The baby wears a crown . . .

'Everyone' is an important word when thinking about celebrations. A good celebration involves everyone, and the very best are the spontaneous celebrations that come when the pressure of feeling is too great to be ignored.

Everyone suddenly burst out singing;
And I was filled with such delight
As prisoned birds must find in freedom
Winging wildly across the white
Orchards and dark green fields; on – on – and out of sight.

Siegfried Sassoon was writing about the response to the end of the First World War. Some celebrations have an undertone of sorrow and at the back of Sassoon's poem lies the appalling experience of the worst conflict up to that point in the history of warfare. Millions, literally, lost their lives in the trenches in futile fighting. Sassoon's poem expresses the sheer relief when the killing finally stopped.

A very large part of religious feeling is the need to celebrate the good things of the earth. 'Glory be to God . . .' seems almost the only response to some of the beauties of the world. Gerard Manley Hopkins, who was a Jesuit priest as well as a poet, wrote some of the best poetry in the language in praise of the Creator. What makes his poetry so good is his lovely observation of things, and his inexhaustible novelty in finding ways of capturing them in words. And not just the obvious things either. In 'Pied Beauty', Hopkins celebrates the mixtures of colours in life – 'pied' means parti-, or multi-coloured. Very few things – certainly very few natural things – are just one colour, and that mixture of colours is one of the things that makes for beauty. Hopkins had as strong a sense of beauty as any other English poet, and he looked at things as carefully as a painter who wants to get his picture just right.

FUNNY FOLK

Welcome to the party
welcome to the fun,
the house is full of funny folk –
there's room for everyone!
meet . . .
my sister Clarissa (but don't try to kiss her!)
my big brother Bert, what's that in his shirt?
my mad Uncle Dan, he's a terrible man,
my Aunty who sings, my Granny with wings,
my friend Emma Hackett, oh what a racket!
There's Herbaceous Plod, he is rather odd,
and Elastic Jones, with his rubber bones,
poor Marjorie Fry (she's swallowed a fly!)
Here's young Henry King, still tongue-tied in string,
Big Gumgo, Giant Jojo,
Jittery Jim and Thin Flynn.
Mrs. Thing-um-e-bob came
with old . . . what's-his-name?
Who's that in the mirror, well riddle-me-ree,
everyone is different, that's plain to see,
(and who could be funnier than you, or me).
The gang's all here, oh what a din!
we're having a party

                    so come on in

                                    Robert Fisher

FROM CARNIVAL TO
CABBAGES AND RAIN

The narrow streets
Are smiles wide
Carnival has come to town.
Granny has a rose in her teeth
The baby wears a crown.
Everyone has come outside
To follow pied piper bands
Wearing dressing up clothes
Dancing hand in hands.
Hearts and blood
Beat to the drum.
Children free balloons –
'I gave mine to the sun'
A child cries.
Strangers are greeted as friends
Under the blue skies.
The streets vibrate
Deep into the night
And rock from end to ends.
Children sleep on parents' shoulders
Late and light
Weaving Carnival into dreams
Round rainbow bends.

They shop for cabbages today
In narrow streets
Polite and grey.
Glitter shines
Down in the drain
And people say
'Now it can rain.'

Julie Holder

WEDDING DAY

Lillian McEever is bride for the day
Wearing Mummy's old wedding dress long locked away
And a posy of dandelions for her bouquet
And a tiara of daisies.

Birdsong showers silver on Institute Drive
Where Lillian waits for her guests to arrive
And the shouts and the laughter shake the morning alive
There's a wedding today.

Past the brook they wind where the cherry trees bloom
Casting white showers of blossom over bride and groom
And grandmothers dream in curtained front rooms
And remember.

Lillian McEever forget not this day
For Spring mornings die but memories stay
When the past like the dress is long locked away
And the leaves fall.

Gareth Owen

HAMNAVOE MARKET

No school today! We drove in our gig to the town.
Grand-da bought us each a coloured balloon.
Mine was yellow, it hung high as the moon.
A cheapjack urged. Swingboats went up and down.

Coconuts, ice-cream, apples, ginger beer,
Routed the five bright shillings in my pocket.
I won a bird-on-a-stick and a diamond locket.
The Blind Fiddler, the broken-nosed boxers were there.

The booths huddled like mushrooms along the pier.
I ogled a goldfish in its crystal cell.
Round every reeling corner came a drunk.

The sun whirled a golden hoof. It lingered. It fell
On a nest of flares. I yawned. Old Madge our mare
Homed through a night black as a bottle of ink.

George Mackay Brown

MARTY'S PARTY

Marty's party?
Jamie came. He
seemed to Judy
dreadful rude. He
joggled Davy,
spilled his gravy,
squeezed a melon
seed at Helen,
gave a poke so
Eddy's Coke so
fresh and fizzy
showered Lizzy;
jostled Frank who
dropped a hank
of juicy candy.
Debby handy –
double bubble
gum in trouble –
Debbie mebbie
stumbled, bumbled
into Jessie
Very messy!
Very sticky!

That's a quickie –
not so ludi-
crous to Judy,
watching Jamie
jilting Amy,
wilting Mamie,
finding Vicky.

What a tricky
lad! Where's Marty?
Don't know. She just
gave the party.

David McCord

FIRSTS

First tinkling laugh,
First wailing cry,
First nagging doubt,
First shameful lie.

First day of school,
First tiny tooth,
First pangs of guilt,
First painful truth.

First white winter morning,
First fresh apple bite,
First star in the sky
On a cool, clear night.

First independence,
First leaving Mum,
First memories,
Firsts still to come.

Zoë Gardner

DRAGON DANCE

A Chinese dragon's in the street
And dancing on its Chinese feet
With fearsome head and golden scale
And twisting its ferocious tail.
Its bulging eyes are blazing red
While smoke is puffing from its head
And well you nervously might ask
What lies behind that fearful mask.
It twists and twirls across the road
While BANG the cracker strings explode.
Don't yell or run or shout or squeal
Or make a Chinese dragon's meal
For, where its heated breath is fired
They say it likes to be admired.
With slippered joy and prancing shoe
Why, you can join the dragon too.
There's fun with beating gongs and din
When dragons dance the New Year in.

Max Fatchen

'IN BEAUTY MAY I WALK'

In beauty	may I walk
All day long	may I walk
Through the returning seasons	may I walk
Beautifully will I possess again	
Beautifully birds	
Beautifully joyful birds	
On the trail marked with pollen	may I walk
With grasshoppers about my feet	may I walk
With dew about my feet	may I walk
With beauty	may I walk
With beauty before me	may I walk
With beauty behind me	may I walk
With beauty above me	may I walk
With beauty all around me	may I walk
In old age, wandering on a trail of beauty,	
lively,	may I walk
In old age, wandering on a trail of beauty,	
living again,	may I walk
It is finished in beauty	
It is finished in beauty	

Anon

From the Navajo (trans. Jerome K. Rothenberg)

EVERYONE SANG

Everyone suddenly burst out singing;
And I was filled with such delight
As prisoned birds must find in freedom
Winging wildly across the white
Orchards and dark green fields; on – on – and out of sight.

Everyone's voice was suddenly lifted,
And beauty came like the setting sun.
My heart was shaken with tears, and horror
Drifted away . . . O, but everyone
Was a bird; and the song was wordless; the singing will never
   be done.

Siegfried Sassoon

PIED BEAUTY

Glory be to God for dappled things –
   For skies of couple-colour as a brinded cow;
     For rose-moles all in stipple upon trout that swim;
Fresh-firecoal chestnut-falls; finches' wings;
   Landscape plotted and pieced – fold, fallow, and plough;
     And áll trádes, their gear and tackle and trim.

All things counter, original, spare, strange;
   Whatever is fickle, freckled (who knows how?)
     With swift, slow; sweet, sour; adazzle, dim;
He fathers-forth whose beauty is past change:
                    Praise him.

Gerard Manley Hopkins

GRANDAD'S BIRTHDAY TREAT

It was me Grandad's birthday
we thought it a treat
to take him to restaurant for something to eat

We found this posh steakhouse
Grandad ordered a steak
a well done chewy-chunky beefcake
(I for one thought it was a dreadful mistake)

And no sooner he began to eat his meat
out jumped his false teeth
landing clean at his feet

Me mum gave me Grandad a family glare
'Grandad didn't I tell ye to have it
soft 'n' rare?'
Grandad didn't turn the tiniest hair

He simply bent down and picked up his teeth
in no time again he was eating his meat
'What a feat,' he murmured quietly to his beard
'What a feat, Lord, bless the courage of my false teeth.'

Grace Nichols

THE BIRTHDAY OF BUDDHA

With my elder brother and younger sister
I, the youngest son, Chaki, aged eleven,
accompany father, mother, elder sister
to the small temple at the end of our street.

At the other end of our street hangs like an old
wood-block print, beyond the grey tiled roofs
of little shops and houses, our divine Mount Fuji –
a lucky omen for this holy day – for Fuji-san
too often hides himself in smog or clouds.
But today the lingering last snows on his sacred peak
are sparkling in the pure blue heavens.

We are all wearing our best clothes –
my mother and sisters in bright spring kimono and zori,
we three men in good suits, shirts, ties, shoes.
But my father's carrying a folding paper fan.

At the temple gate, the smiling priest
bows his welcome, and we all bow deeply in return.
He sometimes plays baseball with us, but today
he is wearing formal robes.

We bow to the statue of the infant Buddha
standing inside his miniature temple
of spring greenery and pale-rose cherry-blossom.
He is shining in the happy sun. One by one,
we slowly pour over him ladles of sweet brown tea.
He always seems to enjoy it. He, too, is smiling.

The priest and his wife and children invite us
to take tea, the same festive tea we gave the Buddha,
with sweet cakes, satsumas and candies.

With folded hands, we bow farewell to Buddha,
and to the smiling priest, who bows farewell to us.

– But once outside the temple gate
my older brother and I dash home to change our clothes
for baseball practice in the field behind the temple,
where the infant Buddha goes on smiling
as if he, too, is on our team.

And at the end of our street, old Fuji-san
hangs like a crimson half-moon in the afterglow.

James Kirkup

CORROBOREE

Hot day dies, cook time comes.
Now between the sunset and the sleeptime
Time of play about.
The hunters paint black bodies by firelight with
    designs of meaning
To dance corroboree.
Now didgeridoo compels with haunting drone
    eager feet to stamp,
Click-sticks click in rhythm to swaying bodies
Dancing corroboree.
Like Spirit things in from the great surrounding
    dark
Ghost-gums dimly seen stand at the edge of
    light
Watching corroboree.
Eerie the scene in leaping firelight,
Eerie the sounds in that wild setting
As naked dancers weave stories of the tribe
Into corroboree.

Kath Walker

COLOUR

Colour

Imagine what it would be like if people couldn't see colours, if your picture of the world was like that on an old black-and-white television set. Without colour how would we know when berries were ripe? Or tell our team from the opposition? In a colour-free world everything would seem the same – flat and dull.

Colour is so important to us, it means much more than simply what our eyes detect. Every colour has its own atmosphere, its own personality and association – so that even people who can't see, can perceive and understand the meaning of colour:

> . . . running water, that is blue;
> And red is like a trumpet sound; and pink
> Is like the smell of roses . . .
>
> *Anon* 'I Asked A Little Boy Who Cannot See'

And we all know the sort of person Jean Binta Breeze is describing when she calls her mother a 'red woman' and the sort of sadness James Berry means when he writes about the 'blues of faces'. You could probably describe your own moods or the whole personality of a friend in a single colour. Do it for a week of ups and downs or for a big group of mates and you'll create a rainbow, the best and boldest show of colour that there is! When you think more about how important colour is to us in how we see and describe the world, you'll start spotting living rainbows everywhere . . . in trees and flowers and animals, inside and outside people no matter what colour their skins seem to be:

> The world is full of
> coloured people
> People of Colour
> Colourful people
> Tra-la-la!
>
> *Alice Walker* 'Song'

You can find rainbows even in the dark, in the sheen of a Jackdaw's wing shining against the black to show how colour needs blackness to set it off:

> poor light
> that has no shadow
> poor white
> that has no black
> poor day without a night
> no dreams to follow

Philip Gross 'Jack's Black Day'

I ASKED THE LITTLE BOY
WHO CANNOT SEE

I asked the little boy who cannot see,
'And what is colour like?'
'Why, green,' said he,
'Is like the rustle when the wind blows through
The forest; running water, that is blue;
And red is like a trumpet sound; and pink
Is like the smell of roses; and I think
That purple must be like a thunderstorm;
And yellow is like something soft and warm;
And white is a pleasant stillness when you lie
And dream.'

Anon

THE PAINT BOX

'Cobalt and umber and ultramarine,
Ivory black and emerald green –
What shall I paint to give pleasure to you?'
'Paint for me somebody utterly new.'

'I have painted you tigers in crimson and white.'
'The colours were good and you painted aright.'
'I have painted the cook and a camel in blue
And a panther in purple.' 'You painted them true.

Now mix me a colour that nobody knows,
And paint me a country where nobody goes,
And put in it people a little like you,
Watching a unicorn drinking the dew.'

E. V. Rieu

NATURAL HIGH

my mother is a
red
woman

she
gets high
on clean children

grows
common sense

injects
tales
with heroines

fumes
over dirty habits

hits the sky
on bad lines

crackling meteors

my mother
gets red
with the sun

Jean Binta Breeze

A BLACK MAN'S SONG

I looked in the mirror.
What did I see?
Not black not white,
but me, only me.

> Coal black face
> with big bright eyes
> and lily white teeth,
> that's lil old me.

Yes I looked in the mirror.
What did I see?
I saw a fella
who's dear to me.

> Short broad nose,
> full thick lips
> and black kinky hair;
> man that's me.

Oh I looked in the mirror.
What did I see?
I saw a fella
as cute as can be,

> that must be me.

If you look
in the mirror
what will you see?

> You may see black,
> you may see white;
> but you won't see me,
> no siree not me.

Jimi Rand

OTHER SIDE OF TOWN

Talking faces
Wear the blues
Of singing faces

Thoughtful faces
Wear the blues
Of vocal faces

Laughing faces
Wear the blues
Of sad faces

Hopeful faces
Wear the blues
Of hopeless faces

Dressed up faces
Wear the blues
Of poverty faces

Sober faces
Wear the blues
Of drunken faces

Praying faces
Wear the blues
Of swearing faces

Love swoon faces
Wear the blues
Of hatestruck faces

Clean free faces
Wear the blues
Of jail faces

O side of town
Your sad faces
Are blues faces

James Berry

GREEN MAN, BLUE MAN

As I was walking through Guildhall Square
I smiled to see a green man there,
But when I saw him coming near
My heart was filled with nameless fear.

As I was walking through Madford Lane
A blue man stood there in the rain.
I asked him in by my front-door,
For I'd seen a blue man before.

As I was walking through Landlake Wood
A grey man in the forest stood,
But when he turned and said, 'Good day'
I shook my head and ran away.

As I was walking by Church Stile
A purple man spoke there a while.
I spoke to him because, you see,
A purple man once lived by me.

But when the night falls dark and fell
How, O how, am I to tell,
Grey man, green man, purple, blue,
Which is which is which of you?

Charles Causley

ORANGES

which came first
the colour or the fruit

. . .

through the archway
a tarnished moon.
in the wicker basket
green oranges huddle
in unweeping melancholy

. . .

in the long grass a ripe
orange, its heart
secretly stolen by ants

. . .

in the tree a young
boy and
the oranges, both
will come down
together

. . .

when they are ready to be picked
the oranges
stop pretending to be leaves

. . .

the orange on the table
drew all the light in the room into it
and still it did not shine

. . .

even in the hand the orange
maintains an air of
resolute inviolability

. . .

her fingers pressed just so hard
into the orange
flesh into flesh
her mind was elsewhere

. . .

the torn skin
shards
of a broken pot

. . .

nothing is shared
as simply as
an orange

Dave Calder

EVENING RED

Evening red and morning grey,
Send the traveller on his way;
Evening grey and morning red
Bring the rain upon his head.

Anon

THE COLOUR

(The following lines are partly original, partly
remembered from a Wessex folk-rhyme)

'What shall I bring you?
Please will white do
Best for your wearing
   The long day through?'
'– White is for weddings,
Weddings, weddings,
White is for weddings,
   And that won't do.'

'What shall I bring you?
Please will red do
   The long day through?'
'– Red is for soldiers,
Soldiers, soldiers,
Red is for soldiers,
   And that won't do.'

'What shall I bring you?
Please will blue do
Best for your wearing
   The long day through?'
'– Blue is for sailors,
Sailors, sailors,
Blue is for sailors,
   And that won't do.'

'What shall I bring you?
Please will green do
Best for your wearing
   The long day through?'
'– Green is for mayings,
Mayings, mayings,
Green is for mayings,
   And that won't do.'

'What shall I bring you
Then? Will black do
Best for your wearing
   The long day through?'
'– Black is for mourning,
Mourning, mourning,
Black is for mourning,
   And black will do.'

Thomas Hardy

YELLOW

Yellow for melons.
Yellow for sun.
Yellow for buttercups,
Picked one by one.

The yolk of an egg
Is yellow, too.
And sometimes clouds
Have a daffodil hue.

Bananas are yellow
And candleshine.
What's your favourite colour?
Yellow is mine.

Olive Dove

JACK'S BLACK DAY

I'm in everybody's black books
Blackguards give me black looks

Black magic   Black arts
Blacklegs with black hearts

Blackmail me in the dark
Blacklisted   Black mark

The black sheep of the family
Black Jack that's me

Black-eyed beaten black-and-blued
Guess the colour of my mood!

★

Tonight, I dreamed I flew
to Africa. No moon, no star
to guide me, I flew into black,
the heart of it. I flew so far.
At dawn I dabbled in a pool

inlaid with pebbles of pure jet.
Among the cool shades of a tree
I saw the Queen of Sheba, black
and strong and smooth as ebony,
a casual hand stretched out to pet

a leashed black panther, deadly-
sleek as an underground stream.
It purred and then, like any black
cat, crossed my path. The queen
bent down to me and said . . .

poor light
that has no shadow
poor white
that has no black
poor day without a night
no dreams to follow

I preen and glisten in the sun, Black Jack.

Philip Gross

CHAMELEONS

Chameleons are seldom seen.
They're red, they're orange, then they're green.
They're one of nature's strangest sights,
Their colours change like traffic lights.

Colin West

THE RAINBOW

The rainbow's like a coloured bridge
that sometimes shines from ridge to ridge.
Today one end is in the sea,
the other's in this field with me.

Iain Crichton-Smith

SONG

The world is full of coloured
people
People of Colour
Tra-la-la
The world is full of
coloured people
Tra-la-la-la-la.

They have black hair
and black and brown
eyes
The world is full of
coloured people
Tra-la-la.

The world is full of coloured
people
People of Colour
Tra-la-la
The world is full of coloured
people
Tra-la-la-la-la.

Their skins are pink and yellow
and brown
All coloured people
People of Colour
Coloured people
Tra-la-la.

Some have full lips
Some have thin
Full of coloured people
People of Colour
Coloured lips
Tra-la-la.

The world is full of
coloured people
People of Colour
Colourful people
Tra-la-la!

Alice Walker

THE GREEN SPRING

When Spring comes
I see the woods turning green,
The water in the river turning green,
The hills turning green,
The beetles turning green,
And even the white-bearded old man turning green.
The green blood
Nurtures the fatigued earth,
And from the earth bursts forth
A green hope.

Shan-Mei

HEROES AND HEROINES

HEROES AND HEROINES

We all have heroes and heroines, men and women we look up to for their special qualities of skill, courage, charisma, intellectual power. The full list of mine would be a long one, but it would include sportsmen like Ian Botham, Jimmy Connors, Bruce Grobbelaar; pop stars like Bob Dylan and Tina Turner; comedians like John Cleese and Rowan Atkinson; writers like Kingsley Amis, Philip Larkin and Ted Hughes. Who your heroes are says quite a lot about who you are – what you particularly like, what qualities you admire in others and which you'd like to develop in yourself.

Clearly one of Brian Lee's heroes is Bobby Charlton. In his poem he offers homage to him, but also tries to express just what it was about Charlton that made him different from a host of other very good footballers.

Sir Walter Scott's 'Young Lochinvar' is another sort of hero – dashing, brave, a brilliant rider, he turns up on his charger to steal away the girl he loves on her wedding day. He scoops her up and onto his horse and leads the groom and his irate father a merry chase over the hills and far away. Hardly a foot wrong, you'd think. But I can't help feeling he may have made a mistake when he declared publicly: 'There are maidens in Scotland more lovely by far, That would gladly be bride to the young Lochinvar.' A bit tactless to say the least.

But modesty and tact are not perhaps qualities to look for in a hero. You certainly won't find them displayed by Toad of Toad Hall, whose splendid Song – grammatical errors and all – gives a dashing self-portrait of one of the most wonderfully, ludicrously self-admiring characters in English literature.

> The clever men at Oxford
>   Know all that there is to be knowed.
> But they none of them know one half as much
>   As intelligent Mr Toad!

If I were to give you my full list of heroes and heroines, the Russian poet, Irina Ratushinskaya would certainly be on it. Under the brutal regime of the old USSR, she was condemned to hard labour camp in Siberia for 'anti-Soviet agitation and propaganda'. Was she a spy? Was she the ring-leader of a group of saboteurs? Was she even an underground political agitator? No, she was a poet. And that's exactly what she continued to be despite a near starvation diet, terrible cold, physical and psychological conditions designed to break her spirit. 'No, I'm not afraid' is just one of the many passionate and powerful poems she wrote during her time behind the barbed wire.

Irina Ratushinskaya was eventually released amidst a media blitz of newspaper reports and television coverage. But you don't have to be on the television or in the newspapers to be heroic. For both Margaret Walker and Maya Angelou, the truly heroic happens at home. It's women who shoulder the burden of keeping the whole human race on the march. If a hero or heroine is a role model, then Margaret Walker's shows who she would like to emulate:

> My grandmothers were strong.
> Why am I not as they?

A SONG OF TOAD

The world has held great Heroes,
　As history-books have showed;
But never a name to go down to fame
　Compared to that of Toad!

The clever men at Oxford
　Know all that there is to be knowed.
But they none of them know one half as much
　As intelligent Mr Toad!

The animals sat in the ark and cried,
　Their tears in torrents flowed.
Who was it said, 'There's land ahead'?
　Encouraging Mr Toad!

The Army all saluted
　As they marched along the road.
Was it the King? Or Kitchener?
　No. It was Mr Toad.

The Queen and her ladies-in-waiting
　Sat at the window and sewed.
She cried, 'Look! who's that *handsome* man?'
　They answered, 'Mr Toad.'

The motor-car went Poop-poop-poop
　As it raced along the road.
Who was it steered it into a pond?
　Ingenious Mr Toad!

Kenneth Grahame

YOUNG LOCHINVAR

O, Young Lochinvar is come out of the west,
Through all the wide Border his steed was the best,
And save his good broadsword he weapons had none;
He rode all unarmed, and he rode all alone.
So faithful in love, and so dauntless in war,
There never was knight like the young Lochinvar.

He stayed not for brake, and he stopped not for stone,
He swam the Eske river where ford there was none;
But, ere he alighted at Netherby gate,
The bride had consented, the gallant came late:
For a laggard in love, and a dastard in war,
Was to wed the fair Ellen of brave Lochinvar.

So boldly he entered the Netherby Hall,
Among bride's-men and kinsmen, and brothers and all:
Then spake the bride's father, his hand on his sword
(For the poor craven bridegroom said never a word),
'O come ye in peace here, or come ye in war,
Or to dance at our bridal, young Lord Lochinvar?'

'I long wooed your daughter, my suit you denied;
Love swells like the Solway, but ebbs like its tide –
And now I am come, with this lost love mine
To lead but one measure, drink one cup of wine.
There are maidens in Scotland more lovely by far,
That would gladly be bride to the young Lochinvar.'

The bride kissed the goblet; the knight took it up,
He quaffed of the wine, and he threw down the cup,
She looked down to blush, and she looked up to sigh,
With a smile on her lips and a tear in her eye.
He took her soft hand, ere her mother could bar,
'Now tread we a measure!' said young Lochinvar.

So stately his form, and so lovely her face,
That never a hall such a galliard did grace;
While her mother did fret, and her father did fume,
And the bridegroom stood dangling his bonnet and plume;
And the bride-maidens whispered, ''Twere better by far
To have matched our fair cousin with young Lochinvar.'

One touch of her hand, and one word in her ear,
When they reached the hall-door, and the charger stood near;
So light to the croupe the fair lady he swung,
So light to the saddle before her he sprung!
'She is won! we are gone, over bank, bush, and scaur;
They'll have fleet steeds that follow,' quoth young Lochinvar.

There was mounting 'mong Graemes of the Netherby clan;
Fosters, Fenwicks, and Musgraves, they rode and they ran;
There was racing, and chasing, on Cannobie Lee,
But the lost bride of Netherby ne'er did they see.
So daring in love, and so dauntless in war,
Have ye e'er heard of gallant like young Lochinvar?

Sir Walter Scott

THE HERO

Slowly with bleeding nose and aching wrists
After tremendous use of feet and fists
He rises from the dusty schoolroom floor
And limps for solace to the girl next door
Boasting of kicks and punches, cheers and noise,
And far worse damage done to bigger boys.

Robert Graves

THE HERO

Say we made a journey, mother,
Roaming far and wide together –
    You would have a palanquin,
    Doors kept open just a chink,
    I would ride a red horse, clip
Clop-clip along beside you, lifting
    Clouds of red dust with my clatter.

Now, suppose it's getting darker,
Suddenly we're blocked by water –
    What a place, how bleak and wild,
    Not a man or beast in sight.
    You take fright, feel in your mind
We're lost. I tell you, 'Don't be frightened,
    Look, we'll take that dried-up river.'

What a thorny, thistly region –
All the cattle have been taken
    Under cover for the night.
    How the path we're taking winds,
    Darkness makes it hard to find –
Then suddenly I hear you crying,
    'Near the water, what's that lantern?'

Next thing shouts and yells surround us,
Figures closing in upon us –
    All four bearers fall away,
    Quake in bushes; you remain
    Crouched in fear, reciting names
Of gods, while I keep calmly saying,
    'I am here, no one shall harm us.'

Just imagine, *lāthi*-wielding
Long-haired desperate villains wearing
  Jabā-flowers behind their ears –
  'Stay right there,' I shout, 'keep clear!
  See this sword? I'll chop you, pierce
Each man who comes one footstep nearer.'
  Still they come, leaping and yelling.

You say, 'No, Oh don't go near them!'
I say, 'Sit tight, I can take them,
  Watch –' I spur my horse, at once
  Swords and bucklers clash and thud –
  Mother, you would faint at such

A fight! Some flee; the rest I scupper
  Somehow: run them through, behead them.

You think they have surely killed me,
All those hefty men against me,
  Till I roll up, smeared with blood,
  Pouring sweat – 'The battle's done,
  Come outside,' I call. You rush
And hug me, kiss me. 'What a lucky
  Thing,' you say, 'that you were with me.'

Life is such a boring matter,
Why are the exciting stories never
  True? How this one would amaze
  Neighbours, brothers – what? such great
  Strength in one so small? My fame
Would spread, with everybody saying,
  'What luck he was with his mother!'

                    Rabindranath Tagore

LINEAGE

My grandmothers were strong.
They followed plows and bent to toil.
They moved through fields sowing seed.
They touched earth and grain grew.
They were full of sturdiness and singing.
My grandmothers were strong.

My grandmothers are full of memories
Smelling of soap and onions and wet clay
With veins rolling roughly over quick hands
They have many clean words to say.
My grandmothers were strong.
Why am I not as they?

Margaret Walker

NO, I'M NOT AFRAID

No, I'm not afraid: after a year
Of breathing these prison nights
I will survive into the sadness
To name which is escape.

The cockerel will weep freedom for me
And here – knee-deep in mire –
My gardens shed their water
And the northern air blows in draughts.

And how am I to carry to an alien planet
What are almost tears, as though towards home . . .
It isn't true, I am afraid, my darling!
But make it look as though you haven't noticed.

Irina Ratushinskaya

WOMAN WORK

I've got the children to tend
The clothes to mend
The floor to mop
The food to shop
Then the chicken to fry
The baby to dry
I got company to feed
The garden to weed
I've got shirts to press
The tots to dress
The cane to be cut
I gotta clean up this hut
Then see about the sick
And the cotton to pick.

Shine on me, sunshine
Rain on me, rain
Fall softly, dewdrops
And cool my brow again.

Storm, blow me from here
With your fiercest wind
Let me float across the sky
'Til I can rest again.

Fall gently, snowflakes
Cover me with white
Cold icy kisses and
Let me rest tonight.

Sun, rain, curving sky
Mountain, oceans, leaf and stone
Star shine, moon glow
You're all that I can call my own.

Maya Angelou

IN PRAISE OF THE BLACKSMITH

Today this place is full of noise and jollity.
The guiding spirit that enables my husband to forge makes
   him do wonders.
All those who lack hoes for weeding, come and buy!
Hoes and choppers are here in plenty.
My husband is a craftsman in iron,
Truly a wizard at forging hoes.
Ah, here they are! They have come eager to find hoes.
Ah, the iron itself is aglow, it is molten red with heat,
And the ore is ruddy and incandescent.
My husband is an expert in working iron,
A craftsman who sticks like wax to his trade.
On the day when the urge to forge comes upon him,
The bellows do everything but speak.
The pile of slag rises higher and higher.
Just look at what has been forged,
At the choppers, at the hoes, at the battle axes,
And here at the pile of hatchets,
Then look at the double-bladed knives and the adzes.
Merely to list them all seems like boasting.
As for fowl and goats, they cover my yard.
They all come from the sale of tools and weapons.
Here is where you see me eating at ease with a spoon.

traditional from the Shona
translated by George Fortune

48

BOBBY CHARLTON

like this: head up, looking where he was going
just as you were supposed to, but always
changing direction, slightly, now this
way, now that, no more than needed so that
obstructions do not have to be met
are not there, simply:
                                        a kind of cunning
for a shy man, nothing as artless as contact,
evasion was mannerly:
                                        head up,
knowing where he was, where the others were
what they were doing, and changing the pattern
with the same flowing unhastening stride:
head up, shoulders back, leaning from the toes,
the same stride with the conscious grace gone
that used to bring him bending in from his wing,
faded into something better, at the centre, experienced
making connections from such a distance . . .

confluence, influence, with the same flow, although
older, slower, the moments were fewer;
one of the best, and better than some of the best,
as good as he could be, and then at last
a refinement of all that he had been: like that.

                                                                Brian Lee

EVERY DAY IN EVERY WAY

(Dr Coue: Every day in every way
I grow better and better)

When I got up this morning
I thought the whole thing through:
Thought, Who's the hero, the man of the day?
Christopher, it's you.

With my left arm I raised my right arm
High above my head:
Said, Christopher, you're the greatest.
Then I went back to bed.

I wrapped my arms around me,
No use counting sheep.
I counted legions of myself
Walking on the deep.

The sun blazed on the miracle,
The blue ocean smiled:
We like the way you operate,
Frankly, we like your style.

Dreamed I was in a meadow,
Angels singing hymns,
Fighting the nymphs and shepherds
Off my holy limbs.

A girl leaned out with an apple,
Said, You can taste for free
I never touch the stuff, dear,
I'm keeping myself for me.

Dreamed I was in heaven,
God said, Over to you,
Christopher, you're the greatest!
And Oh, it's true, it's true!

I like my face in the mirror,
I like my voice when I sing.
My girl says it's just infatuation –
I know it's the real thing.

Kit Wright

THE UNINCREDIBLE HULK-IN-LAW

Being the Incredible Hulk's
scrawny stepbrother ain't easy.
Sticky-fisted toddlers
pick fights with me
in misadventure playgrounds.

On beaches
seven-stone weaklings
kick sand in my eyes
vandalize my pies
and thrash me with candyfloss.

They all tell their friends
how they licked the Hulk . . .
(. . . well not the Hulk exactly,
but an incredibly unincredible relative).

Bullied by Brownies
mugged by nuns
without a doubt
the fun's gone out
of having a T.V. star in the family.

Think I'll marry
Wonderwoman's asthmatic second cousin
and start a commune in Arkansas
for out-of-work, weedy
super heroes-in-law.

Roger McGough

DEMOLITION WORKER

There he is, ten storeys above the street,
Highlighted by his white shirtsleeves,
No hard hat or safety harness
But pick in hand, on top of a narrow peak
Made, not of stone, but of brick.
His way to get from the roof to the ground
Is to knock the building beneath him down,
Like knocking a mountain bit by bit
From underneath your feet
As a means of descending it.
From the way he walks on the wall, pausing to kick
Mortar down with his steel-toed boot,
Everest would seem easy to him.

Stanley Cook

Travel

TRAVEL

People do a lot of dashing about. We hurry into traffic jams, crowded buses and crammed trains twice a day to be moved from one place to another. And once a year we bundle into aeroplanes to take off in one country and plop down into a sunnier one.

All this frantic movement isn't travel. Travel is something much more special, when the journey itself is as important as the arrival. The route doesn't have to be exotic, but it helps . . .

> I should like to rise and go
> Where the golden apples grow;
> Where below another sky
> Parrot islands anchored lie . . .
>
> *Robert Louis Stevenson* 'Travel'

For proper travel I think the mode of transport is important. It's hard to do real travelling by aeroplane because it goes too fast and all you see on the way is clouds. Walking is best, but any vehicle will do so long as you can look around you as you go and appreciate what you see. That way even ordinary everyday journeys can be transformed into travel. Short train trips can be made special just by the wonderful names of the stations.

> From Victoria I can go
> To Pevensey Level and Piddinghoe
> Open Winkins and Didling Hill
> Three Cups Corner and Selsey Bill.
>
> *Eleanor Farjeon* 'Victoria'

Living is the one sort of real travelling that everyone does. The journey from birth to death takes you to a lot of different places and you have to negotiate all sorts of twists, turns and forks in the route.

I shall be telling this with a sigh
Somewhere ages and ages hence:
Two roads diverged in a wood, and I –
I took the one less travelled by,
And it has made all the difference.

Robert Frost 'The Road Not Taken'

Life, like all real travel, is not predictable; adventures and excitement may come at any stage in the journey, even right at the end: as in this story of the old man who thought his travelling days were numbered:

'And what do you do now that you're old?'
I asked of the elderly man.
'I sit on my bed and I twiddle my thumbs
And I snooze,' he replied, 'and I plan
To make my escape from this nursing place
whose matron is strict with a pale pasty face . . .'
'Then come with me now and away we shall race!'
I said to the elderly man
And he jumped out of bed and we ran.

Richard Edwards 'Me and Him'

That is by no means the end of their journey. Read the whole poem and see!

THE TRAVEL BUREAU

All day she sits behind a bright brass rail
Planning proud journeyings in terms that bring
   Far places near; high-coloured words that sing,
'The Taj Mahal at Agra,' 'Kashmir's Vale',
Spanning wide spaces with her clear detail,
   'Sevilla or Fiesole in spring,
   Through the fiords in June'. Her words take wing.
She is the minstrel of the great out-trail.

At half-past five she puts her maps away,
   Pins on a grey, meek hat, and braves the sleet.
A timid eye on traffic. Dully grey
   The house that harbours her in a grey street,
   The close, sequestered, colourless retreat
Where she was born, where she will always stay.

Ruth Comfort Mitchell

VICTORIA

From Victoria I can go
To Pevensey Level and Piddinghoe,
Open Winkins and Didling Hill,
Three Cups Corner and Selsey Bill.
I'm the happiest one in all the nation
When my train runs out of Victoria Station.

But O the day when I come to town
From Ditchling Beacon and Duncton Down,
Bramber Castle and Wisborough Green,
Cissbury Ring and Ovingdean!
I'm the sorriest one in all the nation
When my train runs into Victoria Station.

Eleanor Farjeon

A TRIP TO MORROW

I started on a journey just about a week ago
For the little town of Morrow in the State of Ohio.
I never was a traveller and really didn't know
That Morrow had been ridiculed a century or so.
I went down to the depot for my ticket and applied
For tips regarding Morrow, interviewed the station guide.
Said I, 'My friend, I want to go to Morrow and return
Not later than to-morrow, for I haven't time to burn.'

Said he to me, 'Now let me see, if I have heard you right
You want to go to Morrow and come back to-morrow night,
You should have gone to Morrow yesterday and back
   to-day.
For if you started yesterday to Morrow, don't you see
You should have got to Morrow and returned to-day at three.
The train that started yesterday, now understand me right,
To-day it gets to Morrow and returns to-morrow night.'

'Now if you start to Morrow, you will surely land
To-morrow into Morrow, not to-day you understand,
For the train to-day to Morrow, if the schedule is right
Will get you into Morrow by about to-morrow night.'
Said I, 'I guess you know it all, but kindly let me say,
How can I go to Morrow if I leave the town to-day?'
Said he, 'You cannot go to Morrow any more to-day,
For the train that goes to Morrow is a mile upon its way.'

Anon

TRAVEL

I should like to rise and go
Where the golden apples grow;
Where below another sky
Parrot islands anchored lie,
And, watched by cockatoos and goats,
Lonely Crusoes building boats;
Where in sunshine reaching out
Eastern cities, miles about,
Are with mosque and minaret
Among sandy gardens set,
And the rich goods from near and far
Hang for sale in the bazaar;
Where the Great Wall round China goes,
And on one side the desert blows,
And with bell and voice and drum,
Cities on the other hum;
Where are forests, hot as fire,
Wide as England, tall as a spire,

Where the knotty crocodile
Lies and blinks in the Nile,
And the red flamingo flies
Hunting fish before his eyes;
Where in jungles, near and far,
Man-devouring tigers are,
Lying close and giving ear
Lest the hunt by drawing near,
Or a comer-by be seen
Swinging in a palanquin;

Where among the desert sands
Some deserted city stands,
All its children, sweep and prince,
Grown to manhood ages since,
Not a foot in street or house,
Not a stir of child or mouse,
And when kindly falls the night,
In all the town no spark of light.
There I'll come when I'm a man
With a camel caravan;
Light a flower in the gloom
Of some dusty dining-room;
See the pictures on the walls,
Heroes, fights, and festivals;
And in a corner find the toys
Of the old Egyptian boys.

Robert Louis Stevenson

LET BASIL GO TO BASILDON

Let Basil go to Basildon,
Let Lester go to Leicester;
Let Steven go to Stevenage
With raincoat and sou'wester.

Let Peter go to Peterhead,
Let Dudley go to Dudley;
Let Milton go to Milton Keynes –
The pavements there are puddly.

Let Felix go to Felixstowe,
Let Barry go to Barry;
Let Mabel go to Mablethorpe,
But I at home shall tarry.

Let Alice go to Alice Springs,
Let Florence go to Florence;
Let Benny go to Benidorm
Where rain comes down in torrents.

Let Winnie go to Winnipeg,
Let Sidney go to Sydney;
Let Otto go to Ottawa –
I am not of that kidney.

Let Vera to to Veracruz,
Let Nancy go to Nancy,
But I'll stay home while others roam –
Abroad I do not fancy.

Colin West

UPHILL

Does the road wind uphill all the way?
  Yes, to the very end.
Will the day's journey take the whole long day?
  From morn to night, my friend.

But is there for the night a resting-place?
  A roof for when the slow, dark hours begin.
May not the darkness hide it from my face?
  You cannot miss that inn.

Shall I meet other wayfarers at night?
  Those who have gone before.
Then must I knock, or call when just in sight?
  They will not keep you waiting at that door.

Shall I find comfort, travel-sore and weak?
  Of labour you shall find the sum.
Will there be beds for me and all who seek?
  Yea, beds for all who come.

Christina Rossetti

THE LEGS

There was this road,
And it led up-hill,
And it led down-hill,
And round and in and out.

And the traffic was legs,
Legs from the knees down,
Coming and going,
Never pausing.

And the gutters gurgled
With the rain's overflow,
And the sticks on the pavement
Blindly tapped and tapped.

What drew the legs along
Was the never-stopping,
And the senseless, frightening
Fate of being legs.

Legs for the road,
The road for legs,
Resolutely nowhere
In both directions.

My legs at least
Were not in that rout:
On grass by the roadside
Entire I stood,

Watching the unstoppable
Legs go by
With never a stumble
Between step and step.

Though my smile was broad
The legs could not see,
Though my laugh was loud
The legs could not hear.

My head dizzied, then:
I wondered suddenly,
Might I too be a walker
From the knees down?

Gently I touched my shins.
The doubt unchained them:
They had run in twenty puddles
Before I regained them.

Robert Graves

THREE FRENCH MICE

Three French mice went out for the day –
They went to Paris, but that was too gay.
They went to Bordeaux,
But that was too slow,
They went to Toulouse
And lost their shoes.
They went to Nice
And told the police.
They went to Marseilles
And ate some snails.
But when they got to Spain
They all ran home again.

Translated from French nursery rhyme by Rose Fyleman

THE ANT EXPLORER

Once a little sugar ant made up his mind to roam –
To fare away far away, far away from home.
He had eaten all his breakfast, and he had his Ma's consent
To see what he should chance to see and here's the way he
   went –
Up and down a fern frond, round and round a stone,
Down a gloomy gully where he loathed to be alone,
Up a mighty mountain range, seven inches high,
Through the fearful forest grass that nearly hid the sky,
Out along a bracken bridge, bending in the moss,
Till he reached a dreadful desert that was feet and feet across.
'Twas a dry, deserted desert, and a trackless land to tread;
He wished that he was home again and tucked-up tight in bed.
His little legs were wobbly, his strength was nearly spent,
And so he turned around again and here's the way he went –
Back away from desert lands feet and feet across,
Back along the bracken bridge bending in the moss,
Through the fearful forest grass, shutting out the sky,
Up a mighty mountain range seven inches high,
Down a gloomy gully, where he loathed to be alone,
Up and down a fern frond and round and round a stone,
A dreary ant, a weary ant, resolved no more to roam,
He staggered up the garden path and popped back home.

C. J. Dennis

ROLLING DOWN TO RIO

I've never sailed the Amazon
   I've never reached Brazil;
But the *Don* and *Magdalena*,
   They can go there when they will!

        Yes, weekly from Southampton,
        Great steamers, white and gold,
        Go rolling down to Rio
        (Roll down – roll down to Rio!)
        And I'd like to roll to Rio
        Some day before I'm old!

I've never seen a Jaguar,
   Nor yet an Armadill-
o dilloing in his armour,
   And I s'pose I never will,

        Unless I go to Rio
        These wonders to behold –
        Roll down – roll down to Rio –
        Roll really down to Rio!
        Oh, I'd love to roll to Rio
        Some day before I'm old!

                Rudyard Kipling

THE ROAD NOT TAKEN

Two roads diverged in a yellow wood,
And sorry I could not travel both
And be one traveler, long I stood
And looked down one as far as I could
To where it bent in the undergrowth;

Then took the other, as just as fair,
And having perhaps the better claim,
Because it was grassy and wanted wear;
Though as for that the passing there
Had worn them really about the same,

And both that morning equally lay
In leaves no step had trodden black.
Oh, I kept the first for another day!
Yet knowing how way leads on to way,
I doubted if I should ever come back.

I shall be telling this with a sigh
Somewhere ages and ages hence:
Two roads diverged in a wood, and I –
I took the one less traveled by,
And that has made all the difference.

Robert Frost

THE PEDLAR'S CARAVAN

I wish I lived in a caravan,
With a horse to drive, like a pedlar-man!
Where he comes from nobody knows,
Nor where he goes to, but on he goes.

His caravan has windows two,
With a chimney of tin that the smoke comes through,
He has a wife, and a baby brown,
And they go riding from town to town.

Chairs to mend and delf to sell –
He clashes the basins like a bell.
Tea-trays, baskets, ranged in order,
Plates, with the alphabet round the border.

The roads are brown, and the sea is green,
But his house is just like a bathing machine.
The world is round, but he can ride,
Rumble, and splash to the other side.

With the pedlar-man I should like to roam,
And write a book when I come home.
All the people would read my book,
Just like the Travels of Captain Cook.

W.B. Rands

ME AND HIM

'What did you do when you were young?'
I asked of the elderly man.
'I travelled the lanes with a tortoiseshell cat
And a stick and a rickety van,
I travelled the paths with the sun on a thread,
I travelled the roads with a bucket of bread,
I travelled the world with a hen on my head
And my tea in a watering can,'
Said the elderly, elderly man.

'And what do you do now that you're old?'
I asked of the elderly man.
'I sit on my bed and I twiddle my thumbs
And I snooze,' he replied, 'and I plan
To make my escape from this nursing-home place
Whose matron is strict with a pale pasty face . . .'
'Then come with me now and away we shall race!'
I said to the elderly man
And he jumped out of bed and we ran.

And now we wander wherever we want,
Myself and the elderly man,
With a couple of sticks and a tortoiseshell cat
And a rickety-rackety van,
We travel the paths with the sun on a thread,
We travel the roads with two buckets of bread,
We travel the world with a hen on each head
And our tea in a watering can,
Young me and the elderly man.

Richard Edwards

WAR

WAR

Leaving aside earthquakes, volcanoes, typhoons, drought and other natural disasters, war is the worst thing that can happen. And unlike natural disasters, war is made by man. The history of mankind is very largely the history of conflict. The ingenuity, energy, courage that man has poured into the warfare is one of the most tragic aspects of life on earth. The American poet Carl Sandburg, taking the long view of both the past and the future, doesn't feel optimistic about our ability to cure ourselves of this cycle of destructiveness.

In the old wars kings quarreling and thousands of men
    following.
In the new wars kings quarreling and millions of men
    following.
In the wars to come kings kicked under the dust and millions
    of men following great causes not yet dreamed out in the
    heads of men.

Wars are fought by soldiers. But, beneath their uniforms, soldiers are ordinary men. They suffer loneliness, homesickness, fear, boredom. W.H. Auden's poem 'Roman Wall Blues' is about one of the Roman soldiers on Hadrian's Wall dividing conquered England from the marauding Picts north of the border. He's an exile at the extreme edge of the great Roman empire, and he's fed up. The only way he can cope is by imagining how it will be when he finally gets home and retires:

> When I'm a veteran with only one eye
> I shall do nothing but look at the sky.

Of course in between the long stretches of boredom and homesickness, a soldier has to face the prospect of battle. Waiting to go into battle must be like waiting to go into an exam – only a hundred times worse. Some go into it in a better state of mind than others. Indeed, W.B. Yeats's Irish Airman looks forward with almost complete detachment.

The development of the aeroplane has meant that war has become much more terrible in the 20th century. The chivalrous dog-fights of the First World War gave way to the mass bombing of the Second World War. After suffering the German Blitz in the early days of the war, the British retaliated through Bomber Command. Noël Coward's 'Lie in the Dark and Listen' suggests what it must having been like in bed at night listening to the bombers setting off on another mission:

> Lie in the dark and listen
> They're going over in waves and waves
> High above villages, hills and streams,
> Country churches and little graves
> And little citizens' worried dreams.

Of course with the introduction of bombing, citizens of both sides were brought right into the firing line. In military terms, civilians are 'soft targets'. When I wrote my poem of that title at the start of the Gulf War in January 1991 I was trying to bring home – literally – the common humanity of all of us 'soft targets', whether we happened to be British or Iraqi. It's a war poem without any mention of war at all.

The people who go down in history are the generals, though contrary to Shel Silverstein's engaging fantasy of General Clay and General Gore, they don't get involved in the fighting. That is done by the soldiers, and they are the ones left stretched out on the battlefield afterwards. What was it all for? is a question not often asked by the military historians, let alone, Was it worth it? In Robert Southey's poem 'The Battle of Blenheim', it's the child who questions the morality of war, while the old man who is telling the story of the battle is prepared to go on accepting the old line about 'the famous victory'.

> 'But what good came of it at last?'

is a very good question.

WARS

In the old wars drum of hoofs and the beat of shod feet.
In the new wars hum of motors and the tread of rubber tires.
In the wars to come silent wheels and whirr of rods not yet
dreamed out in the heads of men.

In the old wars clutches of short swords and jabs into faces
with spears.
In the new wars long-range guns and smashed walls, guns
running a spit of metal and men falling in tens and twenties.
In the wars to come new silent deaths, new silent hurlers not
yet dreamed out in the heads of men.

In the old wars kings quarreling and thousands of men
following.
In the new wars kings quarreling and millions of men
following.
In the wars to come kings kicked under the dust and millions
of men following great causes not yet dreamed out
in the heads of men.

Carl Sandburg

SOLDIERS

If you're feeling jaded,
Or if you're feeling blue,
Have a little battle . . .
That's what the soldiers do.

When Genghis Khan was feeling bored
He'd gather up his Golden Horde
And say: 'Today we'll devastate
As far as Kiev.' And they'd say: 'Great!'

A Khan who wants to bring some charm
Into his life will spread some harm.
A little killing, here and there,
Gives life to armies everywhere.

It's very hard, you see, to train
For years in ways of causing pain
Without occasionally trying
Out the latest ways of dying.

The Goths, when life began to pall,
Would simply go and ravage Gaul.
And every Vandal, every Hun,
Agreed on 'How To Have Some Fun'.

Caesar and Napoleon too
Would all do what good soldiers do,
And – who knows – get a little thrill
From giving chaps the chance to kill.

So if you're feeling jaded,
Or if you're feeling blue,
Have a little battle . . .
That's what the soldiers do.

Terry Jones

ROMAN WALL BLUES

Over the heather the wet wind blows,
I've lice in my tunic and a cold in my nose.

The rain comes pattering out of the sky.
I'm a Wall soldier, I don't know why.

The mist creeps over the hard grey stone.
My girl's in Tungria; I sleep alone.

Aulus goes hanging around her place,
I don't like his manners, I don't like his face.

Piso's a Christian, he worships a fish;
There'd be no kissing if he had his wish.

She gave me a ring but I diced it away;
I want my girl and I want my pay.

When I'm a veteran with only one eye
I shall do nothing but look at the sky.

W. H. Auden

SOLDIERS

Brother,
I saw you on a muddy road
in France
pass by with your battalion,
rifle at the slope, full marching order,
arm swinging;
and I stood at ease,
folding my hands over my rifle,
with my battalion.
You passed me by, and our eyes met.
We had not seen each other since the days
we climbed the Devon hills together:
our eyes met, startled;
and, because the order was Silence,
we dared not speak.

O face of my friend,
alone distinct of all that company,
you went on, you went on,
into the darkness;
and I sit here at my table,
holding back my tears,
with my jaw set and my teeth clenched,
knowing I shall not be
even so near you as I saw you
in my dream.

F. S. Flint

THE SECOND WORLD WAR

        The voice said 'We are at War'
And I was afraid, for I did not know what this meant.
My sister and I ran to our friends next door
As if they could help. History was lessons learnt
        With ancient dates, but here

        Was something utterly new,
The radio, called the wireless then, had said
That the country would have to be brave. There was much to
  do.
And I remember that night as I lay in bed
        I thought of soldiers who

        Had stood on our nursery floor
Holding guns, on guard and stiff. But war meant blood
Shed over battle-fields, Cavalry galloping. War
On that September Sunday made us feel frightened
        Of what our world waited for.

Elizabeth Jennings

THE GENERALS

Said General Clay to General Gore,
'Oh *must* we fight this silly war,
To kill and die is such a bore.'
'I quite agree,' said General Gore.

Said General Gore to General Clay,
'We *could* go to the beach today
And have some ice cream on the way.'
'A *grand* idea,' said General Clay.

Said General Clay to General Gore,
'We'll build sand castles on the shore.'
Said General Gore, 'We'll splash and play.'
'Let's go *right now*,' said General Clay.

Said General Gore to General Clay,
'But what if the sea is *closed* today?
And what if the sand's been blown away?'
'A *dreadful* thought,' said General Clay.

Said General Gore to General Clay,
'I've always feared the ocean's spray
And we may drown – it's true, we may,
And we may even drown today.'
'Too true, too true,' said General Clay.

Said General Clay to General Gore,
'My bathing suit is slightly tore,
We'd better go on with our war.'
'I quite agree,' said General Gore.

Then General Clay charged General Gore
As bullets flew and cannon roared.
And now, alas! there is no more
Of General Clay and General Gore.

Shel Silverstein

A DAY IN EARLY SUMMER

A day in early summer
The first year of the war,
Davy Jones and I sat down
By the North Sea-shore.

The sun was bright, warm was the sand,
The sky was hot and blue.
How long we sat there
I never knew:

Rigged in brand-new uniforms,
Two naval sprogs
Dozing in the dancing sun,
Tired as dogs.

Suddenly a child's voice spoke
Across the silent shore:
'Look at those two sailors!
I wonder who they are?'

I sat up and looked about
The yellow and the blue
For the sailors on the shore.
I wondered, too.

Not a seaman could I see
As far as sight could reach:
Only the locked-up pier, the rolls
Of barbed-wire on the beach;

Only the tank-traps on the prom
By the shallow bay;
A woman and a little child
Wandering away;

Only Davy Jones and I
Wearing tiddley suits,
Lanyards, caps with 'HMS',
Shiny pussers' boots.   *naval
                              issue*

God help England, then I thought,
Gazing out to sea,
If all between it and the foe
Is Davy Jones, and me.

Charles Causley

AN IRISH AIRMAN FORESEES
HIS DEATH

I know that I shall meet my fate
Somewhere among the clouds above;
Those that I fight I do not hate,
Those that I guard I do not love;
My country is Kiltartan Cross,
My countrymen Kiltartan's poor,
No likely end could bring them loss
Or leave them happier than before.
Nor law, nor duty bade me fight,
Nor public men, nor cheering crowds,

A lonely impulse of delight
Drove to this tumult in the clouds;
I balanced all, brought all to mind,
The years to come seemed waste of breath,
A waste of breath the years behind
In balance with this life, this death.

W. B. Yeats

LIE IN THE DARK AND LISTEN

Lie in the dark and listen
It's clear tonight so they're flying high
Hundreds of them, thousands perhaps
Riding the icy, moonlit sky
Men, machinery, bombs and maps
Altimeters and guns and charts
Coffee, sandwiches, fleece-lined boots
Bones and muscles and minds and hearts
English saplings with English roots
Deep in the earth they've left below
Lie in the dark and let them go
Lic in the dark and listen.

Lie in the dark and listen
They're going over in waves and waves
High above villages, hills and streams,
Country churches and little graves
And little citizens' worried dreams
Very soon they'll have reached the sea
And far below them will lie the bays
And coves and sands where they used to be
Taken for summer holidays
Lie in the dark and let them go
Lie in the dark and listen.

Lie in the dark and listen
City magnates and steel contractors
Factory workers and politicians
Soft hysterical little actors
Ballet dancers, reserved musicians
Safe in your warm civilian beds
Count your profits and count your sheep
Life is flying over your heads

Just turn over and try to sleep
Lie in the dark and let them go
Theirs is a world you'll never know
Lie in the dark and listen.

Noël Coward

SAID THE GENERAL

Said the General of the Army,
'I think that war is barmy'
So he threw away his gun:
Now he's having much more fun.

Spike Milligan

JUST ANOTHER WAR

On her sideboard
Nan has a picture
Of a young man
In a soldier's uniform
Smiling proudly.

'That's my brother,
Your Uncle Reg,'
She says,
Her voice tinged
With sadness.

'He was killed
In Korea
He was only nineteen.'

'Where's Korea?' I say.
'What were they fighting for?'

'Somewhere in Asia,'
She says.
'I don't know.
It was just another war.'

John Foster

SOFT TARGETS

The church clock strikes the hour: it's
  12 o'clock.
Gloved and scarved against the chill
The pigeon lady comes to feed her flock.
The crusts spill out, and down the pigeons
  spill.
I sip my second coffee and take stock.
A cyclist changes gear to take the hill.

My neighbour comes back with her
  shopping done.
A girl is waiting for a bus.
A jogger is enjoying his lunchtime run.
A couple take a stroll. They could be us,
Chatting as they walk, enjoying the sun.
The day's developing its impetus.

The bus has come: the girl has
  disappeared.
Some laughing schoolgirls cross the road.
They're full of fun, however carefully
  reared.
A carrier staggers underneath his load.
A carpet seller with a grizzled beard
Tots up the sums of money he is owed.

Sandals, slippers, scuff the sandy street
As people take the evening air.
This group are friends who regularly meet
To drink sweet tea together in the square,
Recuperating from the sapping heat.
And then the muezzin calls for evening
  prayer.

[JANUARY 1992]   *Simon Rae*

Muezzin: the call to prayer in Muslim countries.

THE BATTLE OF BLENHEIM

It was a summer evening;
   Old Kaspar's work was done,
And he before his cottage door
   Was sitting in the sun;
And by him sported on the green
His little grandchild Wilhelmine.

She saw her brother Peterkin
   Roll something large and round,
Which he beside the rivulet
   In playing there had found.
He came to ask what he had found,
That was so large, and smooth, and round.

Old Kaspar took it from the boy,
   Who stood expectant by;
And then the old man shook his head,
   And with a natural sigh,
''Tis some poor fellow's skull,' said he,
'Who fell in the great victory.

'I find them in the garden,
   For there's many here about;
And often, when I go to plough
   The ploughshare turns them out;
For many thousand men,' said he,
'Were slain in that great victory.'

'Now tell us what 'twas all about,'
   Young Peterkin, he cries;
And little Wilhelmine looks up
   With wonder-waiting eyes;
'Now tell us all about the war,
And what they fought each other for.'

'It was the English,' Kaspar cried,
   'Who put the French to rout;
But what they fought each other for,
   I could not well make out;
But everybody said,' quoth he,
'That 'twas a famous victory.

'My father lived at Blenheim then,
   Yon little stream hard by;
They burnt his dwelling to the ground,
   And he was forced to fly;
So with his wife and child he fled,
Nor had he where to rest his head.

'With fire and sword the country round
   Was wasted far and wide,
And many a childing mother then,
   And new-born baby, died;
But things like that, you know, must be
At every famous victory.

'They say it was a shocking sight
   After the field was won;
For many thousand bodies here
   Lay rotting in the sun;
But things like that, you know, must be
After a famous victory.

'Great praise the Duke of Marlboro' won,
   And our good Prince Eugene.'
'Why, 'twas a very wicked thing!'
   Said little Wilhelmine.
'Nay, nay, my little girl,' quoth he;
'It was a famous victory.

'And everybody praised the Duke
   Who this great fight did win.'
'But what good came of it at last?'
   Quoth little Peterkin.
'Why, that I cannot tell,' said he;
'But 'twas a famous victory.'

Robert Southey

DIS FIGHTING

No more fighting please, why can't we stop dis fighting,
dis fighting hurting me, why don't we start uniting,
dem fighting in Angola, dem fighting in Manchester,
dem fighting in Jamaica, and dem fighting in Leicester,
well i might be black, my people were once slaves,
but time goes on, and love comes in,
so now we must behave,
it could be that you're white, and i live in your land,
no reason to make war, dis hard fe understand,
skinheads stop dis fighting,
rude boys stop dis fighting,
dreadlocks stop dis fighting,
we must start uniting,
our children should be happy and they should live as one,
we have to live together so let a love grow strong,
let us think about each other, there's no need to compete,
if two loves love each other then one love is complete,
no more fighting please, we have to stop dis fighting,
dis fighting hurting me, time fe start uniting,
dis fighting have no meaning, dis fighting is not fair,
dis fighting makes a profit for people who don't care,
no more fighting please, we have to stop, dis fighting,
dis fighting hurting me, the heathen love dis fighting.

Benjamin Zephaniah

CITIES

CITIES

Cities have a bad reputation. I bet the first five things that the word 'city' makes you think of are bad – Smog . . . Concrete . . . Traffic . . . Rubbish . . . Violence . . . Cities are viewed as human-created blots on the natural world:

Build your houses, build your houses, build your towns,
Fell the woodland, to a gutter turn the brook . . .

F. L. Lucas 'Beleaguered Cities'

That's just the way I used to think. I saw cities as piles of buildings crammed with people who didn't speak to each other. Everyone seemed lonely and separate, but after a while I began to see the patterns of the community in the crowds, the shops and the houses. Amongst the thousands of people coming and going were the core of residents like me, people whose home was the city. I began to see my street as my village. I stopped looking at the dustbins and looked at the trees and the park, I started to enjoy the hum and activity of metropolitan life . . .

When you're out in the city
Shuffling down the street,
A bouncy city rhythm
Starts to boogie in your feet.

Gareth Owen 'Out in the City'

Now I love the way I can run round the corner to drop in on my friends or order a pizza at midnight. I still hate the traffic and the smog and the fights on Saturday nights, but now I see that they don't have to be part of the city. We can clean away the rubbish, we can cut back on cars, we can give people better things to do than beat each other up. Cities can be beautiful and natural, cities can be home for people like birds have nests and rabbits have warrens. Just read the first poem in this section to give you inspiration to imagine what they should, what they *could* be like.

ON WESTMINSTER BRIDGE

Earth has not anything to show more fair:
  Dull would he be of soul who could pass by
A sight so touching in its majesty:
This City now doth like a garment wear
The beauty of the morning; silent, bare,
  Ships, towers, domes, theatres, and temples lie
  Open unto the fields, and to the sky,
All bright and glittering in the smokeless air.
Never did sun more beautifully steep
  In his first splendour valley, rock, or hill;
N'er saw I, never felt, a calm so deep!
  The river glideth at his own sweet will:
Dear God! the very houses seem asleep;
  And all that mighty heart is lying still!

William Wordsworth

CITY RAIN

After the storm
all night before
the world looked like
an upturned mop

wrung out into streets
half-dirty, half-clean,
tasting of rain
in bedraggled trees

and smelling of dog
with its shaky fur
and cold

lick.

Kit Wright

SING A SONG OF PEOPLE

Sing a song of people
   Walking fast or slow;
People in the city
   Up and down they go.

People on the sidewalk,
People on the bus;
People passing, passing,
In back and front of us.
People on the subway
Underneath the ground;
People riding taxis
Round and round and round.

People with their hats on,
Going in the doors;
People with umbrellas
When it rains and pours.
People in tall buildings
And in stores below;
Riding elevators
Up and down they go.

People walking singly,
People in a crowd;
People saying nothing,
People talking loud.
People laughing, smiling,
Grumpy people too;
People who just hurry
And never look at you!

Sing a song of people
   Who like to come and go;
Sing of city people
   You see but never know!

Lois Lenski

DAILY LONDON RECIPE

Take any number of them
you can think of,
pour into empty red bus
                until full,
and then push in
                ten more.
Allow enough time
to get hot under the collar
before transferring into
multistorey building.
Leave for eight hours,
and pour back into same bus
                already half full.
                Scrape remainder off.
When settled down
tip into terraced houses each
carefully lined with copy
of *The Standard* and *Tit Bits*.
Place mixture before open
television screen at 7 p.m.
and then allow to cool
in bed at 10.30 p.m.
May be served with
working overalls
or pinstripe suit.

                                Steve Turner

LIVERPOOL 1988

Ina Liverpool me see de good de bad
de happy and de sad
de history you've had,
Ina Liverpool see me de rich and de poor
most people need more
de future's unsure,
Some move like dem big
Some move move like dem broad
Some like dem massive and dem come from yard,
Is a mixed population
Some bad Police station
People meking money outa race relations.

Ina Liverpool me see de burden bearer
Ex-seafarer, democracy's murder,
Ina Liverpool me see de truth revealing
A militant feeling, bad political dealing.

A city built on slavery
But de everyday person nu have a penny
Yes a very high rate of poverty
And it have a big place in history,

Many actors will put on de accent
Trying to portray the Liverpool experience
Media think its a money making subject
but de soap dat dem mek de people reject,
And plenty people think its cool to visit
but on de journey home dem sey 'I couldn't live in it',
Some will come and just see de city centre
Forget about de ghetto to frighten to enter,
Forget about de people, forget about de evil,
just check places famous for de Beatles
or visit a cathedral to photograph de steeple
it really is incredible cause dem say it wonderful.

Ina Liverpool me see dat and more
Forget de tourist tour
and see what is in store
Ina Liverpool I see a people stan strong
it inspire a song
about what is going on.

Looking at de places where people live
and de so called help dat de government give
mek me think and wonder bout class and race
drive it home dat de state to faced,
when me tink, well me wonder how de people survive
even though so many may commit suicide

You really have to see it, if you see it beware
you can't tell what will happen there,
If you really want to learn bout de North South divide
tek a look round Merseyside
Many people sey Liverpool militant
because no-one heard in de government.

Me is just an observer observing a scene
I could never be an expert if you know what I mean
but I believe Liverpool must be heard
Some things are cool, but some things are absurd

Ina Liverpool me see a colourful people
forget about de Beatles
treat everyone as equal,
I was observing a people who can win
they're made of bones and blood and skin
And London are you listening?

Benjamin Zephaniah

OUT IN THE CITY

When you're out in the city
Shuffling down the street,
A bouncy city rhythm
Starts to boogie in your feet.

It jumps off the pavement,
There's a snare drum in your brain,
It pumps through your heart
Like a diesel train.

There's Harry on the corner,
Sings, 'How she goin' boy?'
To loose and easy Winston
With his brother Leroy.

Shout, 'Hello!' to Billy Brisket
With his tripes and cows heels,
Blood-stained rabbits
And trays of live eels.

Maltese Tony
Smoking in the shade
Keeping one good eye
On the amusement arcade.

And everybody's talking:

Move along
Step this way
Here's a bargain
What you say?
Mind your backs
Here's your stop
More fares?
Room on top.

Neon lights and take-aways
Gangs of boys and girls
Football crowds and market stalls
Taxi cabs and noise.

From the city cafes
On the smoky breeze
Smells of Indian cooking
Greek and Cantonese.

Well, some people like suburban life
Some people like the sea
Others like the countryside
But it's the city
Yes it's the city
It's the city life
For me.

Gareth Owen

AT NIGHT IN THE LAUNDRETTE

I sit in the laundrette
Watch my reflection sitting
On the chequered pavement

The black wet street reflects
Moonmilk, primroses
A bus sails by, a boat
Festooned with lanterns

My shadow warms itself
By a red puddle
Hell's fire flickers there
Stirred by drops of rain

Gerda Mayer

CITY JUNGLE

Rain splinters town.

Lizard cars cruise by;
their radiators grin.

Thin headlights stare –
shop doorways keep
their mouths shut.

At the roadside
hunched houses cough.

Newspapers shuffle by,
hands in their pockets.
The gutter gargles.

A motorbike snarls;
Dustbins flinch.

Streetlights bare
their yellow teeth.
The motorway's
cat-black tongue
lashes across
the glistening back
of the tarmac night.

Pie Corbett

OUR STREET

Our street is not a posh place,

Say the mums in curlers, dads in braces,
   kids in jeans.
Our street is not a quiet place,

Says our football match, our honking bikes,
   our shouts.
Our street is not a tidy place,

Say the lolly wrappers, chippie bags, and
   written-on walls.
Our street is not a lazy place,

Say the car washing dads, clothes washing mums,
   and marbling boys.
Our street is not a short one,

Says milkman Jim, and postman Joe
   and rentman.
Our street is not a new place,

Say the paint-peeled doors, pavements worn,
   and crumbly walls.
Our street is not a green place,

Say the pavements grey, forgotten gardens,
   lines of cars.
But our street is the best

   Says me!

Les Baynton

HIGH STREET SMELLS

A busy street is a public library of smells –
the coffee grinder's fresh aroma at the corner,
the baker's sweet, buttery perfume –
you can almost taste the rolls, the pastries,
and drink the toasted coffee on the morning air.

Out of the sweet shops and the candy stores
oozes the exotic scent of marzipan and chocolate,
and the plebeian breath of chewing gum and
    gobstoppers.
The fruit market is a pungent orchard of
    essential juices,
and my ever-wary nose tells me that I'm approaching
the butcher's, with its plain whiffs of blood and
    sawdust,
while the sea itself comes swimming right
    across the pavement
as I pass the fishmonger's briny bouquets in ice
    and salt.

The Chinese takeaway, the Indian curry restaurant,
the fish-and-chip shop, McDonald's (smell is flavour),
the Olde Worlde Teashoppe, all have their
    distinctive auras
and tangs of sweet and sour, poppadums and spice,
deep-drying oil with vinegar. And toast, cakes
    and tea.

A gush of ironing steam from the laundry. The
  dry cleaner's
sharp, stinging reek, like smelling-salts – what
  a pong!
The pubs are open books of beer, wines and spirits
that my nostrils read rapidly, a kind of boozy braille.
The shoe emporium's rich emanations of supple
  leather, new shoes
impregnating the shoe boxes' pure white
  cardboard and tissue paper.
And here's the newsagent's – you can almost
  read the acrid print
of the local weekly, 'The Farming World,'
  'The People's Friend,'
'Popular Gardening', and all the comics before
  you even open them!
The voluptuous tobacconist's censes with its
  musky leaf
an entire shopping-mall – the drums, cartons
  and boxes
of honeyed shag, and tins of teasing snuff.

These are just some of the olfactory treats
for the aware nostril, the adventurous nose
seeking, among the banal stink and stench of
  exhaust fumes
the characters, the eccentrics, the silent friends
that are the original fragrances of busy streets.

James Kirkup

BELEAGUERED CITIES

Build your houses, build your houses, build your towns,
Fell the woodland, to a gutter turn the brook,
Pave the meadows, pave the meadows, pave the downs,
    Plant your bricks and mortar where the grasses shook,
    The wind-swept grasses shook.
Build, build your Babels black against the sky –
But mark yon small green blade, your stones between,
    The single spy
Of that uncounted host you have outcast;
For with their tiny pennons waving green
    They shall storm your streets at last.

Build your houses, build your houses, build your slums,
    Drive your drains where once the rabbits used to lurk,
Let there be no song there save the wind that hums
    Through the idle wires while dumb men tramp to work,
    Tramp to their idle work.
Silent the siege; none notes it; yet one day
Men from your walls shall watch the woods once more
    Close round their prey.
Build, build the ramparts of your giant-town;
Yet they shall crumble to the dust before
    The battering thistle-down.

F.L. Lucas

ACQUAINTED WITH THE NIGHT

I have been one acquainted with the night.
I have walked out in rain – and back in rain.
I have outwalked the furthest city light.

I have looked down the saddest city lane.
I have passed by the watchman on his beat
And dropped my eyes, unwilling to explain.

I have stood still and stopped the sound of feet
When far away an interrupted cry
Came over houses from another street,

But not to call me back or say good-by;
And further still at an unearthly height,
One luminary clock against the sky

Proclaimed the time was neither wrong nor right.
I have been one acquainted with the night.

Robert Frost

WEATHER

WEATHER

What's the weather like? How often we start the day with that question. Is it cold? Will I need my jumper? Is it going to rain? Will I be too hot in my coat? There are practical reasons for wanting to know. But more importantly, the weather sets the tone for our feelings. A grey day produces grey inside as well, but a brilliantly sunny day brightens up everyone.

Because our weather is so changeable it plays a major part in our life. In less changeable climates people probably talk about it less. After thirty consecutive days of brilliant Mediterranean sun there isn't going to be quite the same excitement as we feel when a drizzling June finally lets up and gives us one perfect summer's day. Unbroken sunlight might even get boring. Linval Quinland certainly suggests that in 'I Can't take the Sun No More, Man'.

> I buy fifty cans of cola,
> I take my clothes off,
> But I'm still hot.

Of course we all like to moan about the weather. Ogden Nash takes a delight in blaming all weather conditions equally, but then he was a humorist. Thomas Hardy writes of the contrast between good weather and bad in his poem 'Weathers', but what I like about this poem especially is how vividly he suggests the wet weather day that he claims not to like. That second stanza is very evocative of a particularly English kind of country wetness.

Henry Wadsworth Longfellow also sees a positive side to the wet.

> How beautiful is the rain!
> How it clatters along the roofs,
> Like the tramp of hoofs!
>
> 'Rain in Summer'

But of course for many people the weather is more than just a matter of inconvenience. Our weather, for all its change-ableness, does give us a very user-friendly climate. Although you wouldn't get many farmers to admit it, our weather doesn't often play complete havoc with the production of the necessities of life. In other parts of the world this isn't the case, and drought is one of the greatest threats to life for many millions of people. In many cultures there are rain gods and the people have to beg them for life-giving rain. 'Rain Song' comes from the North American Pima Indians. It's not so much a direct petition for rain, but an evocation of the coming of rain – as though just jogging the rain gods' memory:

> *Hi-iya, naiho-o!* The earth is rumbling . . .

Out with the umbrellas!

'I CAN'T TAKE THE SUN NO MORE, MAN'

I can't take the sun no more, Man.
I buy fifty cans of cola,
I take my clothes off,
But I'm still hot.
I might as well take off my skin
It's so so so so hot, Man.
I just can't take the sun no more.
I might as well take myself apart
Before the sun melts me.
It's so so so so so so so so so so
Hot, Man.
Just can't take the sun, Man.

Linval Quinland

WHETHER

Whether the weather be fine
Or whether the weather be not
Whether the weather be cold
Or whether the weather be hot –
We'll weather the weather
Whatever the weather
Whether we like it or not!

Anon

WEATHERS

This is the weather the cuckoo likes,
   And so do I;
When showers betumble the chestnut spikes,
   And nestlings fly:
And the little brown nightingale bills his best,
And they sit outside at *The Traveller's Rest*,
And maids come forth sprig-muslin drest,
And citizens dream of the south and west,
   And so do I.

This is the weather the shepherd shuns,
   And so do I:
When beeches drip in browns and duns,
   And thresh, and ply;
And hill-hid tides throb, throe on throe,
And meadow rivulets overflow,
And drops on gate-bars hang in a row,
And rooks in families homeward go,
   And so do I.

Thomas Hardy

IT'S NEVER FAIR WEATHER

I do not like the winter wind
That whistles from the North.
My upper teeth and those beneath,
They jitter back and forth.
Oh, some are hanged, and some are skinned,
And others face the winter wind.

I do not like the summer sun
That scorches the horizon.
Though some delight in Fahrenheit,
To me it's deadly pizen.
I think that life would be more fun
Without the simmering summer sun.

I do not like the signs of spring,
The fever and the chills,
The icy mud, the puny bud,
The frozen daffodils.
Let other poets gaily sing;
I do not like the signs of spring.

I do not like the foggy fall
That strips the maples bare;
The radiator's mating call,
The dank, rheumatic air;
I fear that taken all in all,
I do not like the foggy fall.

The winter sun, of course, is kind,
And summer's wind a saviour,
And I'll merrily sing of fall and spring
When they're on their good behavior.
But otherwise I see no reason
To speak in praise of any season.

Ogden Nash

RAIN IN SUMMER

How beautiful is the rain!
After the dust and heat,
In the broad and fiery street,
In the narrow lane,
How beautiful is the rain!
How it clatters along the roofs,
Like the tramp of hoofs!

How it gushes and struggles out
From the throat of the overflowing spout!
Across the window pane
It pours and pours;
And swift and wide,
With a muddy tide,
Like a river down the gutter roars
The rain, the welcome rain!

Henry Wadsworth Longfellow

GLASS FALLING

The glass is going down. The sun
Is going down. The forecasts say
It will be warm, with frequent showers.
We ramble down the showery hours
And amble up and down the day.
Mary will wear her black galoshes
And splash the puddles on the town;
And soon on fleets of macintoshes
The rain is coming down, the frown
Is coming down of heaven showing
A wet night coming, the glass is going
Down, the sun is going down.

Louis MacNiece

WINDS LIGHT TO DISASTROUS

As I sipped morning tea,
A gale (force three)
Blew away a slice of toast.
Then a gale (force four)
Blew my wife out the door,
I wonder which I'll miss the most.
She was still alive
When a gale (force five)
Blew her screaming o'er Golders Green,
When a gale six blew
And it took her to
A mosque in the Medanine.
Now I pray to heaven
That a gale (force seven)
Will whisk her farther still,
Let a gale (force eight)
Land her on the plate
Of a cannibal in Brazil.
As I sat down to dine
A gale (force Nine)
Blew away my chips & Spam
But! a gale (force ten)
Blew them back again,
What a lucky man I am!

Spike Milligan
Bayswater 1977

RAIN SONG

Hi-iya, naiho-o! The earth is rumbling
From the beating of our basket drums.
The earth is rumbling from the beating
Of our basket drums, everywhere
humming.
Earth is rumbling, everywhere raining.

Hi-iya, naiho-o! Pluck out the feathers
    From the wing of the eagle and turn
them
Toward the east where lie the large
clouds.
    Hi-iya, naiho-o! Pluck out the soft down
From the breast of the eagle and turn it
    Toward the west where sail the small
clouds.
Hi-iya, naiho-o! Beneath the abode
    Of the rain gods it is thundering;
Large corn is there. *Hi-iya, naiho-o!*
    Beneath the abode of the rain gods
It is raining; small corn is there.

Pima Indians, North America

This song was thought to produce rain. The feathers and
down of the eagle represent the gathering clouds.

THE WIND IN A FROLIC

The wind one morning sprung up from sleep,
Saying, 'Now for a frolic! now for a leap!
Now for a mad-cap, galloping chase!
I'll make a commotion in every place!'
So it swept with a bustle right through a great town,
Creaking the signs, and scattering down
Shutters; and whisking, with merciless squalls,
Old women's bonnets and gingerbread stalls.
There never was heard a much lustier shout,
As the apples and oranges trundled about;
And the urchins, that stand with their thievish eyes
For ever on watch, ran off each with a prize.

Then away to the field it went blustering and humming,
And the cattle all wondered whatever was coming;
It plucked by their tails and grave, matronly cows,
And tossed the colts' manes all about their brows,
Till, offended at such a familiar salute,
They all turned their backs, and stood sullenly mute.
So on it went, capering and playing its pranks:
Whistling with reeds on the broad river's banks;
Puffing the birds as they sat on the spray,
Or the traveller grave on the king's highway.
It was not too nice to hustle the bags
Of the beggar, and flutter his dirty rags:
'Twas so bold, that it feared not to play its joke
With the doctor's wig, or the gentleman's cloak.
Through the forest it roared, and cried gaily, 'Now,
You sturdy old oaks, I'll make you bow!'
And it made them bow without more ado,
Or it cracked their great branches through and through.

Then it rushed like a monster on cottage and farm,
Striking their dwellers with sudden alarm;
And they ran out like bees in a midsummer swarm.
There were dames with their 'kerchiefs tied over their caps,
To see if their poultry were free from mishaps;
The turkeys they gobbled, the geese screamed aloud,
And the hens crept to roost in a terrified crowd;
There was rearing of ladders, and logs laying on
Where the thatch from the roof threatened soon to be gone.

(But the wind had passed on, and had met in a lane,
With a schoolboy, who panted and struggled in vain;
For it tossed him, and twirled him, then passed, and he stood,
With his hat in a pool, and his shoe in the mud.)

(There was a poor man, hoary and old,
Cutting the heath on the open wold –
The strokes of his bill were faint and few,
Ere this frolicsome wind upon him blew;
But behind him, before him, about him it came,
And the breath seemed gone from his feeble frame;
So he sat him down with a muttering tone,
Saying, 'Plague on the wind! was the like ever known?
But nowadays every wind that blows
Tells one how weak an old man grows!')

But away went the wind in its holiday glee;
And now it was far on the billowy sea,
And the lordly ships felt its staggering blow,
And the little boats darted to and fro.
But lo! it was night, and it sank to rest,
On the sea-bird's rock, in the gleaming west,
Laughing to think, in its fearful fun,
How little of mischief it had done.

William Howitt

WINTER

When icicles hang by the wall,
   And Dick the shepherd blows his nail,
And Tom bears logs into the hall,
   And milk comes frozen home in pail;
When blood is nipped, and ways be foul
Then nightly sings the staring owl
              Tu-who;
  Tu-whit, tu-who – a merry note,
  While greasy Joan doth keel the pot.

When all aloud the wind doth blow,
   And coughing drowns the parson's saw,
And birds sit brooding in the snow,
   And Marian's nose looks red and raw,
When roasted crabs hiss in the bowl,
Then nightly sings the staring owl
              Tu-who;
  Tu-whit, tu-who – a merry note,
  While greasy Joan doth keel the pot.

William Shakespeare

HURRICANE

Under low black clouds
the wind was all
speedy feet, all horns and breath,
all bangs, howls, rattles,
in every hen house,
church hall and school.

Roaring, screaming, returning,
it made forced entry, shoved walls,
made rifts, brought roofs down,
hitting rooms to sticks apart.

It wrung soft banana trees,
broke tough trunks of palms.
It pounded vines of yams,
left fields battered up.

Invisible with such ecstasy
with no intervention of sun or man –
everywhere kept changing branches.

Zinc sheets are kites.
Leaves are panic swarms.
Fowls are fixed with feathers turned.
Goats, dogs, pigs,
all are people together.

Then growling it slunk away
from muddy, mossy trail and boats
in hedges and cows, ratbats, trees,
fish, all dead in the road.

James Berry

IF I COULD ONLY TAKE
HOME A SNOWFLAKE

Snowflakes
like tiny
insects
drifting down.

Without a hum
they come,
Without a hum
they go

Snowflakes
like tiny
insects
drifting
down.

If only
I could take
one
home with me
to show
my friends
in the sun,
just for fun,
just for fun.

John Agard

WILDFOWL

WILDFOWL

Wildfowl is a funny old-fashioned sort of word. Strictly speaking it means ducks, geese and swans, but all sorts of other water birds creep under its wings . . . flamingos, herons, egrets, coots and moorhens and more. I find that all those watery sort of birds have a special place in my heart, but geese and ducks are my favourites.

One of the most magical things about wild geese is that they migrate, far to the north in spring and back to our coasts and lakes in autumn. They sense the change of seasons before we do and their lovely wild voices mark the borders of winter.

> Something told the wild geese
>   It was time to fly –
> Summer sun was on their wings,
>   Winter in their cry.

Rachel Field 'Something Told the Wild Geese'

Ducks migrate too, but they seem less remote and mysterious than geese . . . lovable, homely, even funny. There is something about the rounded compact shapes, the busy swimming and wobbly walking of ducks that I find irresistible. I had the chance to share my enthusiasm during a *Talking Poetry* writing workshop at Slimbridge. The poet Philip Gross, a classful of children, Simon Rae and I all trooped off on a perfect spring day to collect some poem raw material. There were so many clear and accurate observations made that day that I began to think that all Ornithologists should take a course in poetry writing . . .

> I notice
> a laundry of landed swans
> flapping like shirts
> on a clothes horse . . .

Simon Rae 'Wildfowl Workshop'

We took some of the poems in this section of *Welcome to the Party* with us to read on that day and they describe some of the many sorts of wildfowl we saw, perfectly. I bet you'll recognize this bird even before you read the poem's title . . .

> She's policing the water-bugs
> In her municipal uniform.
> A watchful clockwork
> Jerks her head ahead, to inspect ahead . . .
>
> *Ted Hughes*

It's not rare and you can see one on any park pond. Go on, guess!

THE WILD SWANS AT COOLE

The trees are in their autumn beauty,
The woodland paths are dry,
Under the October twilight the water
Mirrors a still sky;
Upon the brimming water among the stones
Are nine-and-fifty swans.

The nineteenth autumn has come upon me
Since I first made my count;
I saw, before I had well finished,
All suddenly mount
And scatter wheeling in great broken rings
Upon their clamorous wings.

I have looked upon those brilliant creatures,
And now my heart is sore.
All's changed since I, hearing at twilight,
The first time on this shore,
The bell-beat of their wings above my head,
Trod with a lighter tread.

Unwearied still, lover by lover,
They paddle in the cold,
Companionable streams or climb the air;
Their hearts have not grown old;
Passion or conquest, wander where they will,
Attend upon them still.

But now they drift on the still water,
Mysterious, beautiful;
Among what rushes will they build,
By what lake's edge or pool
Delight men's eyes when I awake some day
To find they have flown away?

W.B. Yeats

MALLARD

Squawking they rise from reeds into the sun,
climbing like furies, running on blood and bone,
with wings like garden shears clipping the misty air,
four mallard, hard winged, with necks like rods
fly in perfect formation over the marsh.

Keeping their distance, gyring, not letting slip the air,
but leaping into it straight like hounds or divers,
they stretch out into the wind and sound their horns again.

Suddenly siding to a bank of air unbidden
by hand signal or morse message of command
downsky they plane, sliding like corks on a current,
designed so deftly that all air is advantage,

till, with few flaps, orderly as they left earth,
alighting among curlew they pad on mud.

Rex Warner

THE DUCK

Behold the duck.
It does not cluck.
A cluck it lacks.
It quacks.
It is specially fond
Of a puddle or a pond.
When it dines or sups,
It bottoms ups.

Ogden Nash

WILDFOWL WORKSHOP

for Philip Gross

I notice
a laundry of landed swans
flapping like shirts
on a clothes horse;

a duck taking off
from the grey runway of the estuary,
parting from her reflection
like a pair of dividers . . .

I notice
the flamingos,
marinated the colour of tandoori chicken,
elbowing like crooks
to display waistcoats
of flashy contraband.

I notice
the Indian rope trick
a jet-trail lazily weaves
through the moorhen-wavy water

and the dribble of seeds
dropped to detonate
a squabbling explosion
of geese . . .

I notice
the photographer,
uncorking his black jeraboam
to drink long at the breeding lake
with his one thirsty eye,

but not,
hunched still as a heron,
the poet
– till he snaps open
his notebook and stabs at a
glittering haiku.

Simon Rae

PREENING SWAN

On the green canal the swan
made a slow-motion
swan-storm of itself:
wings moved through wrong angles,
feathers stared, neck
forgot its bones
and a rotted figleaf of a foot
paddled in the air.

Then – one last shrugging ruffle
and everything fell into place,
into stillness, into a classic
hauteur. – The washerwoman
put on an aristocracy
as false as any other one
and, head high, stared at the ridiculous world
through invisible lorgnettes.

Norman MacCaig

THE MOORHEN

Might not notice you.
She's policing the water-bugs
In her municipal uniform.

A watchful clockwork
Jerks her head ahead, to inspect ahead
At each deep tread
Of her giant, ooze-treading claw-spread.

Her undertail flirts, jerk by jerk,
A chevron blaze, her functionary flash,
And thc blood-orange badge or bleb
On her helmet neb
Lets the transgressing water-skeeter know
The arresting face, the stabbing body-blow
Is official.

Her legs are still primaeval,
Toy-grotesque
As when she – this thistledown, black, tiptoe –
Scootered across the picture-skin of water.

Lumpier now, she hurdle-strides into flight
Across stepping stones of slapped circles

Then dangles her drape of webs below her
Like a hawthorn fly, till she hoicks up
Clear over the bull-rush plumes, and crash-drops

Into her off-duty nervous collapse.

Ted Hughes

POEM WITH A GREBE

6.30 a.m.,
the sun pressed into a damp sky.
   Below the blot
willows, willow-pattern,
pylons like pylons
in an otherwise explicable landscape.

   The water is blank.
I am tempted to leave it out altogether
as if a field had been pulled apart
spilling moorhens into nothing at all.
They nod miraculously across the page.
Reed hand in a vacuum.

Till Tom comes, down the cleaving,
a king in his court of water,
Tom from his eel-nets
followed by water.
   He leads the river back.
passes in a litter of light.

The page is crammed with words.
They bob, they bow, they dance after him,
they race along the bank, barking.
   They exhaust themselves.
His ranks already are in disarray,
his brilliants scattering.

Line by line the poem falls asleep,
now at a rat-hole,
now by the bole of a tree,
its mind still turning
a kaleidoscope of white,
   one grebe.

Desmond Heath

THE WILD DUCK

                        got up with a cry
Shook off her Arctic swaddling

Pitched from the tower of the North Wind
And came spanking across water

The wild duck, fracturing egg-zero,
Left her mother the snow in her shawl of stars
Abandoned her father the black wind in his beard of stars

Got up out of the ooze before dawn

Now hangs her whispering arrival
Between earth-glitter and heaven-glitter

Calling softly to the fixed lakes

As earth gets up in the frosty dark, at the back of the Pole Star
And flies into dew
Through the precarious crack of light

Quacking Wake Wake

Ted Hughes

WILD GEESE

Beating their wings
Against the white clouds
You can count each one
Of the wild geese flying:
Moon, an autumn night.

Traditional, Japan

EGRETS

Once as I travelled through a quiet evening,
I saw a pool, jet-black and mirror-still.
Beyond, the slender paperbarks stood crowding;
each on its own white image looked its fill,
and nothing moved but thirty egrets wading –
thirty egrets in a quiet evening.

Once in a lifetime, lovely past believing,
your lucky eyes may light on such a pool.
As though for many years I had been waiting,
I watched in silence, till my heart was full
of clear dark water, and white trees unmoving,
and, whiter yet, those thirty egrets wading.

Judith Wright

SOMETHING TOLD THE WILD GEESE

Something told the wild geese
It was time to go.
Though the fields lay golden
Something whispered, 'Snow.'
Leaves were green and stirring,
Berries, luster-glossed,
But beneath warm feathers
Something cautioned, 'Frost.'
All the sagging orchards
Steamed with amber spice,
But each wild breast stiffened
At remembered ice.
Something told the wild geese
It was time to fly –
Summer sun was on their wings,
Winter in their cry.

Rachel Field

SCHOOL

SCHOOL

Love it or loathe it, there's no escape from school. Compulsion always breeds resentment, even rebellion. We hate having to do things very largely because we have to do them:

> Homework moanwork
> Cross it out and groanwork

On the other hand, writing stories, finding out about the world, and doing experiments are not in themselves boring. But although the teacher's dream world of a nice quiet class of pupils busily getting on with their work does exist – somewhere – it isn't that side of school that inspires poems.

Of course all poets have been to school (and many – the fools – even become teachers), so it's familiar territory to them. Michael Rosen clearly wasn't the teacher's pet. In 'I was Mucking About in Class' he vividly describes the way he exploits the hapless Mr Brown's verbal slip to make the situation even more of a shambles.

Even when not mucking about in class, people spend quite a bit of their time with their mind on other things. I used to look out over the cricket field and daydream about the wickets I was going to take when the summer came. That's probably why I failed Economics.

What do we remember from school? Well, not a very great deal of what we're taught. Latin, French, Maths, Geography, German, Physics, Chemistry – I hate to think how many hours I spent supposedly learning these subjects, and those teachers who tried to teach me them would be appalled if they knew how little has actually stuck. On the other hand, I could probably tell you the names of most of the people in my class, and certainly describe the most memorable. School is the time when, whether we like it or not, we meet other people. From the first day at school, we're thrown in at the deep end, as Barry Heath shows in his poem of that title. And some people stand out like sore thumbs:

Timothy Winters comes to school
With eyes as wide as a football-pool,
Ears like bombs and teeth like splinters;
A blitz of a boy is Timothy Winters.

Describing people is an important part of a poet's job. Is there anyone at your school you could paint in words? (Portraits don't have to be flattering.)

Every school is unique. It has its own atmosphere, its own particular accoustics, its own special smells. You could take me back to my old school blindfold, and I'd know exactly where I was. Gareth Owen's poem 'Our School' concentrates on the things that give the place its own special character. Why not do the same for your school? Love it or loathe it, it will remain with you in your memory for the rest of your life.

SCHOOL BELL

Nine o'Clock Bell!
Nine o'Clock Bell!
All the small children and big ones as well,
Pulling their stockings up, snatching their hats,
Checking and grumbling and giving back-chats,
Laughing and quarrelling, dropping their wings,
These at a snail's pace and those upon wings,
Lagging behind a bit, running ahead,
Waiting at corners for lights to turn red,
Some of them scurrying,
Others not worrying,
Carelessly trudging or anxiously hurrying,
All through the streets they are coming pell-mell
At the Nine o'Clock
Nine o'Clock
Nine o'Clock

Bell!

Eleanor Farjeon

FIRST DAY AT SCHOOL

it wurorribul m'fost
day at school
memate jeff flewit
went wime
an teacha wunt lerrus
sit next tureachother

went shiwent aht
cockut class cumup
t'me
ansed, 'AH canfaityo
cahnt ah?'
an ah sed eecudunt
an ee sed ee cud
an ah sed ee cuddunt
an eeit me
so ah itim back just
as teacha cumin

shipicked up that
stick as y'point
at bord'we
an crackt m'ovver
edweeit
an sed, 'Widontav
ooligunsere.'

so ah went omm at
playtime an towd
memam
an meman took meback
t'school agen
owdin metab.

Barry Heath

OUR SCHOOL

I go to Weld Park Primary,
It's near the Underpass
And five blocks past the Cemetery
And two roads past the Gas
Works with the big tower that smells so bad
   me and me mates put our hankies over our
      faces and pretend we're being attacked
         by poison gas . . . and that.

There's this playground with lines for rounders,
And cricket stumps chalked on the wall,
And kids with their coats for goalposts
Booting a tennis ball
Around all over the place and shoutin' and arguin'
   about offside and they always kick it over
      the garden wall next door and she
         goes potty and tells our head teacher
         and he gets right ratty with
            everybody and stops us playin'
              football . . .
               . . . and everything.

We have this rule at our school
You've to wait till the whistle blows
And you can't go in till you hear it
Not even if it snows
And your wellies get filled with water and your socks
   go all soggy and start slipping down your legs
      and your hands get so cold they go all
         crumpled and you can't undo
         the buttons of your mac when
            you do get inside . . .
             . . . it's true.

The best thing is our classroom.
When it's fine you can see right far,
Past the Catholic Cathedral
Right to the Morris Car
Works where me Dad works as a fitter and sets off
    right early every morning in these overalls
        with his snap in this sandwich box and
            a flask of tea and always moanin'
                about the money . . . honest.

In Hall we pray for brotherly love
And sing hymns that are ever so long
And the Head shouts at Linda Nutter
Who's always doing wrong.
She can't keep out of trouble because
    she always talkin'
        she can't stop our teacher says she
            must have been injected with
                a gramophone needle she talks
                    so much and
that made me laugh once
not any more though I've heard it
    too often . . . teachers!

Loving your enemy sound all right
Until you open your eyes
And you're standing next to Nolan
Who's always telling lies
About me and getting me into trouble and about
    three times a week I fight him after school
        it's like a habit I've got
            but I can't love him even though
                I screw my eyes up real hard and try like
                    mad, but if it wasn't him it
                        would be somebody else

            I mean
        you've got to have enemies . . .
            . . . haven't you?

We sing 'O to be a pilgrim'
And think about God and heaven
And then we're told the football team lost
By thirteen goals to seven
But that's not bad because St Xavier's don't half have
  big lads in their team and last time we played
    they beat us eighteen one and this time
      we got seven goals . . .
        . . . didn't we?

Then we have our lessons,
We have Science and English and Maths,
Except on Wednesday morning
When our class goes to the baths
And it's not half cold and Peter Bradberry's
  fingers went all wrinkled and blue last week
    and I said, 'You're goin' to die, man'
      but he pushed me under the water and I had to
      hold my breath for fifteen minutes.
        But he's still alive though . . .
          . . . he is.

Friday's my favourite day though,
We have Art all afternoon
And I never care what happens
'Cos I know it's home-time soon
And I'm free for two whole days but I think
  sometimes it wouldn't be half so good
    having this weekend if we didn't have five
      days
        of
          school
           in
             between –
Would it?

Gareth Owen

DAYDREAMER

'Aljenard, Winston, Frederick,
Spencer, wha ya look out the winda sa?'
'Me alook pun the nice green grass!'
'But why do you look apun the nice green grass?'
'Me na no!'

'Aljenard, Winston, Frederick Spencer,
wha are ya look out the winda sa?'
'Me alook pun the bright blue sky!'
'But why do you look apun the bright blue sky?'
'Me na no!'

'Aljenard, Winston, Frederick,
Spencer, what are ya look out the winda sa?'
'Me alook pun the hummin burd!'
'But why do you look apun the hummin burd?'
'Ma na no!'

'Aljenard, Winston, Frederick,
Spencer, what are you look out the winda sa?'
'Me alook apun the glistening sun!'
'But why you look apun the glistening sun?'
'Me na no!'

'Aljenard, Winston, Frederick,
Spencer, wha are you look out the winda sa?'
'Me a try to feel the nice warm eir!'
'But why do you try to feel the nice warm eir?'

'Cause me a daydreamer!'

David Durham

THE SONG OF THE HOMEWORKERS

To be read or chanted with increasing velocity

Homework moanwork
Cross it out and groanwork
Homework neatwork
Keeps you off the streetwork
Homework moanwork
Cross it out and groanwork
Homework roughwork
When you've had enoughwork
Homework moanwork
Cross it out and groanwork
Homework dronework
Do it on your ownwork
Homework moanwork
Cross it out and groanwork

Homework gloomwork
Gaze around the roomwork
Homework moanwork
Cross it out and groanwork
Homework guesswork
Book is in a messwork
Homework moanwork
Cross it out and groanwork
Homework rushwork
Do it on the buswork
Homework moanwork
Cross it out and groanwork
Homework hatework
Hand your book in latework
Homework moanwork
Cross it out and groan groan GROANWORK

Trevor Millum

'I WANT A WORD WITH YOU LOT . . .'

'I want a word with you lot,'
The new teacher said.
Out came the butter,
The knife and the bread,
'We hope the word's tasty,'
The cheeky class said.
'We hope it's not SPROUT,
Or CABBAGE or FISH,
(Or anything healthy poured into a dish).
A good word would be
SAUSAGE, or CHOCOLATE, or PIE,
And CAKE is a word
For which we'd all die.'

'Enough of this nonsense!
I'm fed up, I'm through!
You'll all eat your words
When I'm finished with you.
The word that I want
Is not one word, but two
That when stuck together
Make you feel blue.
You all know it well,
You loathe it, you shirk
From facing up to
That word
            HOMEWORK.'

Brian Patten

TIMOTHY WINTERS

Timothy Winters comes to school
With eyes as wide as a football-pool,
Ears like bombs and teeth like splinters:
A blitz of a boy is Timothy Winters.

His belly is white, his neck is dark,
And his hair is an exclamation mark.
His clothes are enough to scare a crow
And through his britches the blue winds blow.

When teacher talks he won't hear a word
And he shoots down dead the arithmetic-bird,
He licks the patterns off his plate
And he's not even heard of the Welfare State.

Timonthy Winters has bloody feet
And he lives in a house on Suez Street,
He sleeps in a sack on the kitchen floor
And they say there aren't boys like him any more.

Old man Winters like his beer
And his missus ran off with a bombardier,
Grandma sits in the grate with a gin
And Timothy's dosed with an aspirin.

The Welfare Worker lies awake
But the law's as tricky as a ten-foot snake,
So Timothy Winters drinks his cup
And slowly goes on growing up.

At Morning Prayers the Headmaster helves
For children less fortunate than ourselves,
And the loudest response in the room is when
Timothy Winters roars 'Amen!'

So come one angel, come on ten:
   Timothy Winters says 'Amen'
      Amen amen amen amen.
         Timothy Winters, Lord.

                              Amen.

                  Charles Causley

I KNOW YOU WOULDN'T
THINK I'M SERIOUS

'Teacher, Teacher,
There's an egg in the computer!'
                              the child cried.

'Teacher, Teacher,
There's an egg on the piano,'
                              the child cried.

'Teacher, Teacher
Look! An egg is on the blackboard,'
                              the child cried.

The teacher sighed
and told the child to stand
outside the headmaster's office.

Just then the headmaster burst into the class.
He was laughing and wringing his hands
and saying to the teacher

'I know you wouldn't think I'm serious,
but do you know there's an egg standing outside my door?'

                              John Agard

THE GHOST

I am the Ghost of School.
I lie
in secret places,
silently.
A mist of chalk dust
films my eye,
and every surface
of my skin
welcomes the mute, sad
ink stain in.

Each stark initial here
is mine:
carved crookedly
on cupboard door
and desk and chair . . .
scratched on the slim
long panels
of the echoing gym
and on the Art room's
painted floor.

I am the past
of boys who come
and go, but no one
calls my name:
each year, I have
a different one –
am in a different
image cast –
yet stay eternally
the same.

Jean Kenward

I WAS MUCKING ABOUT IN CLASS

I was mucking about in class

Mr Brown said,
Get out and take your chair with me
I suppose he *meant* to say
Take your chair with you
so Dave said,
Yeah – you heard what he said
         get out and take my chair with him
so Ken said,
Yeah – get out and take his chair with me
so I said to Mr Brown
Yessir – shall I take our chair with you, sir?

Wow
That meant BIG TROUBLE

Michael Rosen

BIRTH AND DEATH

BIRTH AND DEATH

We are all part of a story, the story of our own life. And like any good story life has a beginning, a middle and an end.

We take the part of all the characters in our story, the baby, the child, the adult, and lots of others along the way, son, daughter, sister, brother, wife, husband, parent. In our one life we become a lot of people.

> All the world's a stage
> And all the men and women merely players:
> They have their exits and their entrances;
> And one man in his time plays many parts,
>
> *William Shakespeare*

We have no control over the beginning of our story; our parents have to write that part for us and sometimes even they don't know how dramatic it will be; a new life has a big effect on the other lives around it . . . sisters and brothers in particular.

> She blind, she dumb, she ugly, she bald,
> She smelly and she cyaan understan',
> A wish mama would tek her back
> An' buy one different one.
>
> *Valerie Bloom* 'New Baby'

Of all the dramas in our life story, death is the greatest. You can never be prepared for the death of someone you love and for the hole in your own story when it can no longer include that person.

> I thought
> I could deal with funerals
> that is until Gran died . . .
>
> *Wes Magee* 'Until Gran Died'

Yet despite the shock and the grief, a death close to you makes life more vivid, even if at the time it is painful. However sad we feel about the death of someone we loved, however frightened in the knowledge that one day we too will die, there is a rightness in death; like winter before spring, death makes space for new life.

> Have ye never a tear to shed
> Nor sigh to drop for the newly-dead,
> Nor marble grief to mark his grave? –
> No, none of these; but see we have
> Green seed to mingle with his earth –
> What, is not this a burying? – Nay, a birth.

Eleanor Farjeon 'A Burying'

ALL THE WORLD'S A STAGE

                              All the world's a stage
And all the men and women merely players:
They have their exits and their entrances;
And one man in his time plays many parts,
His acts being seven ages. At first the infant,
Mewling and puking in the nurse's arms.
Then the whining schoolboy, with his satchel
And shining morning face, creeping like snail
Unwillingly to school. And then the lover,
Sighing like furnace, with a woeful ballad
Made to his mistress's eyebrow. Then a soldier,
Full of strange oaths, and bearded like the pard,
Jealous in honour sudden and quick in quarrel,
Seeking the bubble reputation
Even in the cannon's mouth. And then the justice,
In fair round belly with good capon lined,
With eyes severe and beard of formal cut,
Full of wise saws and modern instances;
And so he plays his part. The sixth age shifts
Into the lean and slippered pantaloon,
With spectacles on nose and pouch on side,
His youthful hose, well saved, a world too wide
For his shrunk shank; and his big manly voice,
Turning again toward childish treble, pipes
And whistles in his sound. Last scene of all,
That ends this strange eventful history,
Is second childishness and mere oblivion,
Sans teeth, sans eyes, sans taste, sans every thing.

William Shakespeare

BIRTH

On the hottest, stillest day of the summer
A calf was born in a field
At Pant-y-Cetris; two buzzards
Measured the volume of the sky;
The hills brimmed with incoming
Night. In the long grass we could see
The cow, her sides heaving, a focus
Of restlessness in the complete calm,
Her calling at odds with silence.

The light flowed out leaving stars
And clarity. Hot and slippery, the scalding
Baby came, and the cow stood up, her cool
Flanks like white flowers in the dark.
We waited while the calf struggled
To stand, moved as though this
Were the first time. I could feel the soft sucking
Of the new-born, the tugging pleasure
Of bruised reordering, the signal
Of milk's incoming tide, and satisfaction
Fall like a clean sheet around us.

Gillian Clarke

WHERE DID THE BABY GO?

I cannot remember –
And neither can my Mother –
Just when it was our baby
Turned into my brother.

Julie Holder

MY LITTLE BROTHER

My mother had a baby,
  And my friends were quick to
say,
'That's the end of all your fun –
  You won't forget this day.'

They said he'd be a nuisance,
  He'd be a smelly pest,
He'd tire out my mum and dad . . .
  Oh, I forget the rest.

It's turned out very different;
  It wasn't lots of bother.
In fact, the truth is simple:
  I *like* my little brother.

He's lots of fun to play with,
  He crawls about and smiles.
I like to take him to the park
  And push him round for miles.

My parents do look tired,
  But I haven't been ignored,
And though we're very busy,
  We're never, ever bored.

My friends all think I'm stupid,
  That something's wrong with me;
Boys don't like babies, they all say.
  Well, I think differently.

I don't care what my friends think,
  Or say to one another;
I'm glad mum had our baby –
  I *like* my little brother.

Tony Bradman

NEW BABY

Mi baby sista come home las' week
An' little most mi dead,
When mama pull back de blanket
An' me see de pickney head.

Couple piece a hair she hab pon i'
An de little pickney face
Wrinkle up an crease up so,
It was a real disgrace.

Mi see har a chew up mama chest
So mi gi' har piece o' meat,
Mama tek i' whey, sey she cyaan eat yet
For she no hab no teeth.

Mi tell mama fi put har down
Mek she play wid mi blue van,
She sey Yvonne cyaan siddung nor stan' up yet
Nor hol' tings eena har han'.

Mi sey a' right but maybe
She can play 'I spy' wid mi,
She tell mi de pickney cyaan talk yet
An she can hardly see.

Aldoah she no hab no use,
An she always wet har bed,
Mi wouldn't mine so much ef she neva
Mek so much nize a mi head.

Every night she wake mi up;
But a mama mi sorry fah,
For everytime she wake up
She starts fi eat mama.

She blind, she dumb, she ugly, she bald,
She smelly, she cyaan understan',
A wish mama would tek har back
An' buy one different one.

Valerie Bloom

BIRTH

I didn't ask
to be born.
I wasn't even
there to ask.
When you are born
you can ask for
anthing.
Almost anything.
You cannot ask
to be unborn.
If you do
there is very little
that can be done.
I didn't ask
to be born.
I was under age
at the time.
My parents had
to decide
on my behalf.
I'm glad that
I was born.
You have to be born
to be glad.

Steve Turner

GRANDAD

Grandad's dead
And I'm sorry about that.

He'd a huge black overcoat
He felt proud in it.
You could have hidden
A football crowd in it.
Far too big –
It was a lousy fit
But Grandad didn't
Mind a bit.
He wore it all winter
With a squashed black hat.

Now he's dead
And I'm sorry about that.

He'd got twelve stories.
I'd heard every one of them
Hundreds of times
But that was the fun of them:
You knew what was coming
So you could join in.
He'd got big hands
And brown, grooved skin
And when he laughed
It knocked you flat.

Now he's dead
And I'm sorry about that.

Kit Wright

A RECOLLECTION

My father's friend came once to tea.
He laughed and talked. He spoke to me.
But in another week they said
That friendly pink-faced man was dead.

'How sad . . .' they said, 'the best of men . . .'
So I said too, 'How sad'; but then
Deep in my heart I thought, with pride,
'I know a person who has died.'

Frances Cornford

MY AUNT SHE DIED A MONTH AGO

My aunt she died a month ago,
And left me all her riches,
A feather-bed and a wooden leg,
And a pair of calico breeches;
A coffee pot without a spout,
A mug without a handle,
A baccy box without a lid,
And half a farthing candle.

Anon

149

UNTIL GRAN DIED

The minnows I caught
lived for a few days in a jar
then floated side-up on the surface.
We buried them beneath the hedge.
I didn't cry, but felt sad inside.

I thought
I could deal with funerals,
that is until Gran died.

The goldfish I kept in a bowl
passed away with old age.
Mum wrapped him in newspaper
and we buried him next to a rose bush.
I didn't cry, but felt sad inside.

I thought
I could deal with funerals
that is until Gran died.

My cat lay stiff in a shoe box
after being hit by a car.
Dad dug a hole and we buried her
under the apple tree.
I didn't cry, but felt *very* sad inside.

I thought
I could deal with funerals,
that is until Gran died.

And when she died
I went to the funeral
with relations dressed in black.
They cried, and so did I.
Salty tears ran down my face. Oh, how I cried.

Yes, I thought
I could deal with funerals,
that is until Gran died.

She was buried in a graveyard
and even the sky wept that day.
Rain fell and fell and fell,
and thunder sobbed far away across the town.
I cried and I cried.

I thought
I could deal with funerals,
that is until Gran
died.

Wes Magee

A BURYING

I see the twelve fair months go by
Bearing a coffin shoulder-high.
What, laughing? Pretty pall-bearers,
Pitiless of the buried years,
Have ye never a tear to shed
Nor sigh to drop for the newly-dead,
Nor marble grief to mark his grave? –
No, none of these; but see, we have
Green seed to mingle with his earth. –
What, is not this a burying? – Nay, a birth.

Eleanor Farjeon

DEATH IN LEAMINGTON

She died in the upstairs bedroom
  By the light of the ev'ning star
That shone through the plate glass window
  From over Leamington Spa.

Beside her the lonely crochet
  Lay patiently and unstirred,
But the fingers that would have work'd it
  Were dead as the spoken word.

And Nurse came in with the tea-things
  Breast high 'mid the stands and chairs –
But Nurse was alone with her own little soul,
  And the things were alone with theirs.

She bolted the big round window,
  She let the blinds unroll,
She set a match to the mantle,
  She covered the fire with coal.

And 'Tea!' she said in a tiny voice
  'Wake up! It's nearly *five*.'
Oh! Chintzy, chintzy cheeriness,
  Half dead and half alive!

Do you know that the stucco is peeling?
  Do you know that the heart will stop?
From those yellow Italianate arches
  Do you hear the plaster drop?

Nurse looked at the silent bedstead,
  At the gray, decaying face,
As the calm of a Leamington ev'ning
  Drifted into the place.

She moved the table of bottles
  Away from the bed to the wall;
And tiptoeing gently over the stairs
  Turned down the gas in the hall.

Sir John Betjeman

MAMA DOT I

Born on a sunday
in the kingdom of Ashante

Sold on monday
into slavery

Ran away on tuesday
cause she born free

Lost a foot on wednesday
when they catch she

Worked all thursday
till her head grey

Dropped on friday
where they burned she

Freed on saturday
in a new century

Fred D'Aguiar

INDEX OF POETS

Index of poems

ACKNOWLEDGEMENTS

The compiler and publishers would like to thank the following for their kind permission to reproduce copyright material:

John Agard c/o Caroline Sheldon Literary Agency for 'I Know You Wouldn't Think I'm Serious' from *Laughter is an Egg*, published by Kestrel/Puffin, 1990 and 'If I Could Only Take Home a Snowflake' from *I Din Do Nuttin*, published by The Bodley Head, 1983; Angus & Robertson (Australia) for 'Egrets' by Judith Wright from her *Collected Poems* © 1971; Les Baynton for 'Our Street'; Bloodaxe Books for 'No, I'm Not Afraid' by Irina Ratushinskaya, trans. by David McDuff © 1986; Valerie Bloom for 'New Baby'; Curtis Brown Ltd for 'It's Never Fair Weather' by Ogden Nash © 1933; Dave Calder for 'Oranges' © 1979 from *The Batik Poems* (Toulouse Press); Carcanet Press Ltd for 'Birth' by Gillian Clarke from *Selected Poems*; Century Hutchinson (Random Century Group) for 'A Recollection' by Frances Cornford from her *Collected Poems*; Chatto & Windus (Random Century Group) for 'Mama Dot I' by Fred D'Aguiar from *Mama Dot*; Chatto & Windus (Random Century Group) for 'Preening Swan' by Norman MacCaig from *Collected Poems*; Pie Corbett for 'City Jungle' © 1989, first published in *Toughie Toffee*, ed. by David Orme (Lions, 1989); Iain Crichton-Smith for 'The Rainbow'; Andre Deutsch Ltd for 'The Duck' by Ogden Nash from *I Wouldn't Have Missed It*; Faber & Faber Ltd for 'Roman Wall Blues' by W. H. Auden from *W. H. Auden: Collected Poems*; Faber & Faber Ltd for 'Jack's Black Day' by Philip Gross from his *Manifold Manor*; Faber & Faber Ltd for 'The Wild Duck' by Ted Hughes from his *Moortown*; Faber & Faber Ltd for 'Glass Falling' by Louis MacNeice from *The Collected Poems of Louis MacNeice*; Robert Fisher for 'Funny Folk' from *Funny Folk* ed. by Robert Fisher, published by Faber & Faber Ltd; John Foster for 'Just Another War' from *Another Fourth Poetry Book*, published by Oxford University Press; The Estate of Robert Frost for 'Acquainted with the Night' and 'The Road Not Taken' by Robert Frost from *The Poetry of Robert Frost*, published by Jonathan Cape; The June Hall Literary Agency (Peters, Fraser & Dunlop Ltd) for 'Other Side of Town by James Berry from *Chain of Days*, published by Oxford University Press; Hamish Hamilton Children's Books (Penguin Group) for 'Hurricane' by James Berry from *When I Dance* by James Berry © 1988; HarperCollins Publishers for 'Wedding Day' by Gareth Owen from *Song of the City* © Gareth Owen 1985, published by Fontana Lions, an imprint of HarperCollins Publishers Ltd; David Higham Associates Ltd for 'A Day in Early Summer' and 'Green Man, Blue Man' by Charles Causley from *Figgie Hobbin*, published by Macmillan; David Higham Associates for 'Timothy Winters' by Charles Causley from his *Collected Poems*, published by Macmillan; David Higham Associates Ltd for 'A Burying' and 'School Bell' by Eleanor Farjeon from *The Children's Bells*, published by Oxford University Press; David Higham Associates Ltd for 'Victoria' by Eleanor Farjeon from *Silver Sand and Snow*, published by Michael Joseph; David Higham Associates for 'The Second World War' by Elizabeth Jennings; David Higham Associates Ltd for 'Song' by Alice Walker from *Horses Make The Landscape More Beautiful*, published by The Women's Press, 1985; Hodder and Stoughton Ltd for 'Daily London Recipe' and 'Birth' by Steve Turner from *Up to Date*; Julie Holder for 'From Carnival to Cabbages and Rain' and 'Where Did the Baby Go'; Hutchinson's Children's Books (Random Century Group) for 'Chameleons' by Colin West from *Not to be Taken Seriously*; Hutchinson's Children's Books (Random Century Group) for 'Let Basil Go to Basildon' by Colin West from *What Would You Do with a Wobble-de-Woo?*; Ted Hughes for 'The Moorhen'; John Johnson (Author's Agent) Ltd for 'Dragon Dance' © Max Fatchen, 1989; Jean Kenward for 'The Ghost' from *School's Out* ed. by John Foster, published by Oxford University Press; James Kirkup for 'The Birthday of Buddha' © 1989 from *Let's Celebrate* ed. by John Foster, published by Oxford University Press and 'High Street Smells' from *Toughie Toffee*, published by HarperCollins; Brian Lee for 'Bobby Charlton'

from *A Puffin Sextet of Poets*, published by Puffin Books; The Lois Lenski Covey
Foundation Inc for 'Sing a Song of People' by Lois Lenski; Wes Magee for 'Until Gran
Died' from *Morning Break and Other Poems*, published by Cambridge University
Press, 1989; Little, Brown and Company for 'Marty's Party' by David McCord from
One at a Time by David McCord © 1974; Sarah Matthews for 'Demolition Worker' by
Stanley Cook from *Another Third Poetry Book* ed. by John Foster, published by
Oxford University Press; Julia MacRae, Publisher, for 'Beleaguered Cities' by F. L.
Lucas from *Shades of Green* ed. by Anne Harvey; Gerda Mayer for 'At Night in the
Laundrette' from *The Knockabout Show* published by Chatto & Windus, 1978;
Methuen (London) for 'Lie in the Dark and Listen' by Noël Coward from his *Collected
Poems*; Spike Milligan Productions Ltd for 'Said the General' from *Silly Verse for Kids*
and 'Winds Light to Disastrous' © 1981 from *Unspun Socks from a Chicken's Laun-
dry*, published by Michael Joseph Ltd; Trevor Millum for 'The Song of the Homewor-
kers' from *Warning – Too Much School Can Damage Your Health*, published by
Nelson; John Murray (Publishers) Ltd for 'Death in Leamington' by John Betjeman;
John Murray (Publishers) Ltd for 'Hamnavoe Market' by George Mackay Brown from
his *Voyages*; Grace Nichols for 'Grandad's Birthday Treat' from *Another Second Poetry Book*, published by Oxford University Press; Gareth Owen for 'Out in the City'
from *Song of the City*; Oxford University Press for 'In Praise of the Blacksmith' ©
1979, reprinted by Shona Praise Poetry, compiled by Aaron C. Hodza, ed. and trans.
by George Fortunc (1979); Brian Patten for 'I Want a Word with You Lot . . .'; Pavi-
lion for 'Soldiers' by Terry Jones from *The Curse of the Vampire's Socks*; Penguin
Books Ltd for 'My Little Brother' by Tony Bradman from *All Together Now* © Tony
Bradman, 1989, published by Kestrel/Puffin; Penguin Books Ltd for 'I Was Mucking
About in Class' by Michael Rosen from *Nine O'Clock Bell* by Raymond Wilson,
published by Viking Kestrel/Puffin; Penguin Books Ltd for 'The Hero' from *Rabindra-
nath Tagore: Selected Poems*, trans. by William Radice © 1985; Penguin Books Ltd for
'Wild Geese' from *The Penguin Book of Japanese Verse* by Geoffrey Bownas and
Anthony Thwaite © 1964; Peters, Fraser & Dunlop for 'The Unincredible Hulk-in-
Law' by Roger McGough from *Sky in the Pie*, published by Penguin Books Ltd; Linval
Quinland for 'I Can't Take the Sun No More, Man' from *A World of Poetry* ed. by
Michael Rosen; Race Today for 'Natural High' by Jean Binta Breeze from *Ryddim
Ravings and other poems*; Simon Rae for 'Soft Targets' and 'Wildfowl Workshop'; Jimi
Rand for 'A Black Man's Song'; Richard Rieu for 'The Paint Box' by E. V. Rieu from
A Puffin Quartet of Modern Poets, published by Puffin; Rogers, Coleridge and White
Ltd for 'Our School' by Gareth Owen from his *Salford Road Poems*; George T. Sass-
oon for 'Everyone Sang' by Siegfried Sassoon; Shel Silverstein for 'The General' from
Where the Sidewalk Ends, published by Jonathan Cape; The Society of Authors as the
Literary Representative for the Estate of Rose Fyleman for 'Three French Mice';
Virago Press Ltd for 'Woman Work' by Maya Angelou from *And Still I Rise* © Maya
Angelou 1978; the Estate of Rex Warner for 'Mallard' from his *Poems*, published by
The Bodley Head; A. P. Watt Ltd on behalf of the Trustees of the Robert Graves
Copyright Trust for 'The Hero' and 'The Legs' from his *Collected Poems*, 1975; the
Watts Group for 'Me and Him' by Richard Edwards from his *A Mouse in my Roof*,
published by Orchard Books, 1988; Jacaranda Wiley Ltd for 'Corroboree' by Kath
Walker from *My People*; Kit Wright for 'City Rain', 'Every Day in Every Way' and
'Grandad'; Benjamin Zephaniah for 'Dis Fightin' and 'Liverpool 1988'.

The compiler and publisher have made every effort to trace copyright holders of
material reproduced in this anthology. If however, they have inadvertently made any
ommission or error, they would be grateful for notification.